TEACHING
IN THE
SMALL COLLEGE

TEACHING
IN THE
SMALL COLLEGE
Issues and Applications

Edited by Richard A. Wright
and John A. Burden

87 - 1184

Contributions to the Study of Education
Number 17

Greenwood Press
New York • Westport, Connecticut • London

Library of Congress Cataloging-in-Publication Data

Main entry under title:

Teaching in the small college.

(Contributions to the study of education,
ISSN 0196–707X; no. 17)
Bibliography: p.
Includes index.
1. Small colleges—United States—Addresses, essays,
lectures.   2. College teaching—United States—
Addresses, essays, lectures.   I. Wright, Richard A.
(Richard Alan), 1953–   .   II. Burden, John A.
III. Series.
LB2328.3.T42   1986   378'.125   85–24850
ISBN 0–313–24662–9 (lib. bdg. : alk. paper)

Library of Congress Catalog Card Number: 85–24850
ISBN: 0–313–24662–9
ISSN: 0196–707X

First published in 1986

Greenwood Press, Inc.
88 Post Road West
Westport, Connecticut 06881

Printed in the United States of America

The paper used in this book complies with the
Permanent Paper Standard issued by the National
Information Standards Organization (Z39.48–1984).

10 9 8 7 6 5 4 3 2 1

For Sharon, William Everett, Emerson Taylor, and Ruth Wright; Judy, Tyson, and Victoria Burden; and our students.

Contents

Acknowledgments

In the spring of 1984 we hosted a conference dealing with "Teaching in the Small College" for faculty and administrators from small colleges in Kansas, Nebraska, and Oklahoma. The participants of this conference reinforced our belief in the need for this book, and we are indebted to them in many ways. Five of the chapters in this book are revisions of papers presented at the confrence. We would like to thank the following people for contributing in significant ways to the success of the conference: Bill Gleason, Dale Goldsmith, Jeff Gundy, Calra B. Howery, G. J. Ikenberry, Jr., Richard E. Owens, Liam Purdon, Richard S. Rempel, William E. Roweton, Sister Mary Faith Schuster, Jan Van Asselt, Jan P. Vermeer, Jeanne Williams, and Joseph J. Wydeven.

Several persons deserve particular thanks for assisting in the completion of the book. Mary Glenzinski, of the Council of Independent Colleges, and John Minter provided some essential national data on small colleges. Also, the staff of Greenwood Press—including James T. Sabin, Maureen Melino, Neil Kraner, Elizabeth Hovinen, and Joan F. Reiss—provided us with helpful support and guidance.

Finally, Norma Tucker, Vice President for Academic Services at McPherson College, deserves special thanks for her moral and financial support for both the conference and the book. She believes, as we do, that there is much good yet to be discovered about small colleges.

TEACHING
IN THE
SMALL COLLEGE

1

Introduction

JOHN A. BURDEN

The time has come to examine teaching in the small college. In terms of study, the small college is perhaps the most neglected of all American institutions of learning. There is almost no empirical literature on small colleges, and descriptions in speculative writing and essays range from denouncements of small colleges as "academic Siberia" (Mandell, 1977:80) to praise for them as something tantamount to "our hope for the future" (Martin, 1982—see Rosecrance, 1962; and Astin and Lee, 1971 for more moderate assessments). Those of us who teach in the small college are aware of the conflicting images. We experience occasional deprecation ("If he were really good, he wouldn't be *there*"), but also admiration for our dedication to teaching. Confusion is to be expected when there is a lack of data and critical examination. In the case of the small college, however, confusion may be costly.

Concerns about institutional survival are very common and apparently justified by demographic and economic factors (Mayhew, 1979). Some small colleges have recently closed, and many others face serious faculty retrenchment. Lower birthrates in the 1960s have resulted in a shrinking pool of persons in the traditional college-attending age brackets in the 1980s.

Also, these young persons are under increasing economic pressures of ever higher tuition and related costs while having less certainty about state and federal financial assistance. Small private colleges with their higher tuition rates invariably lose in the cost comparison with less expensive state universities. As an example of the manifestation of these problems, it is predicted that the pool of available students in Kansas will decline by 25 percent from 1980 to 1990. Of the twenty small private four year colleges in Kansas, fourteen have experienced slight to substantial declines in total headcount enrollments from 1981 to 1984 (P.W. Hoffman, 1985).

Small colleges also represent a minority of all American institutions of higher education. Of the 3,253 colleges and universities listed with the National Center for Educational Statistics (1983–84), there are 476 colleges that are small by our definition (fewer than 1,500 students). Of the approximately 600,000 professors in the United States, about 23,000 or 3.8 percent are full-time small college faculty (Minter, 1985). Why should we care about the fate of small colleges?

All the contributors to this volume share at least one thing in common: We all have considerable teaching and/or consulting experience in a small college setting. This book is intended primarily for those persons who would endeavor to teach in the small college and who, therefore, have an obvious selfish interest in seeing small colleges survive and even flourish. However, there may be other good reasons to be interested in this "small" sector of academe.

A survey of the literature on problems in higher education reveals a common theme: It is a disservice to our society to emphasize research-oriented graduate education to the neglect of basic baccalaureate preparation (see for example Dressel and Marcus, 1982; Martin, 1982; National Institute of Education, 1984; Association of American Colleges, 1985). Some of the main recommendations being offered to improve baccalaureate education are to:

1. *Return to a basic curriculum.* We are more likely to be able to teach universals in depth by emphasizing general education and core courses while avoiding curriculum sprawl brought on by a preoc-

cupation with specialization or course marketability. As one report asks, "Does it make sense for a college to offer a thousand courses to a student who will only take 36?" (Association of American Colleges, 1985)

2. *Put the profession of teaching before the profession of research.* It is revealing that faculty speak of teaching *loads* and research *opportunities.* Training for teaching should be as important as training for research.

3. *Staff the basic and beginning courses with the best and most experienced professors.* The function of graduate assistants should be to *assist.*

4. *Tighten requirements and monitor student learning on an individual basis.*

5. *Involve students in learning.* Large lecture halls with 300 students listening to a public address system cannot be considered excellent higher education. More personal contact between faculty and students is needed—more small discussion groups, informal "bull" sessions, and individual guidance on student-conducted projects.

6. *Present higher education in an intellectual moral/ethical context.* For example, it is not enough to learn *how* to use technology—it is also necessary to learn *when* it should be used.

7. *Revitalize liberal education.* All bachelor's programs should include at least two years of liberal arts courses (National Institute of Education, 1984).

Of all institutions of higher learning, small liberal arts colleges probably have the best potential to fulfill these recommendations. Small colleges have traditionally emphasized both close working relationships between professors and students and teaching as the most important faculty responsibility. And yet, many faculty teaching in small colleges are either not aware of or do not appreciate the potential of their institutions. They may feel "down and out in academia" (Morreale, 1972), because prestige comes to a professor for:

1. Research activities

2. Affiliation with a large school

3. Affiliation with a highly selective school, but more rarely for
4. The professor's (or the school's) impact on students (see McGee, 1971).

TEACHING AND RESEARCH

Although the topic has been debated for some time, there seems to be little empirical relationship between teaching and research abilities—some productive researchers are exciting and effective teachers, others are not (Friedrich and Michalak, 1983; R.A. Hoffman, 1984). College faculty are initially trained to be researchers in spite of the fact that most come to teach as their primary professional activity. As long as there are no clear criteria for evaluating teaching or research effectiveness (reliance on students to evaluate teachers and number of publications to evaluate researchers has been frequently decried as inadequate—see Goldsmid and Wilson, 1980), the relative importance of each will continue to be debated. Many chapters in this volume are concerned with the teaching/research debate (see Chapters 2, 3, 7, 8, 10, and 12). One thing seems clear: Good teaching demands a great deal of time, and until there are significant reductions in teaching loads for small college faculty (not likely), a carefully considered choice must be made. One of the purposes of this book is to add to the continuing discussion of this important issue.

SIZE OF THE SCHOOL

"Bigger is better" is not only part of the American ethos in general, but it also affects institutions of higher learning in particular. In his assessment of prestige rankings among American colleges and universities, McGee (1971) notes that size is probably *the* major factor determining institutional prestige. Large schools seem to have more of everything—more students, more faculty, more classrooms, more microscopes, and usually more advanced and expensive technical equipment. The quantitative advantages of large schools often outshine the qualitative advantages of smaller schools. When their faculty and staff argue that the small college has more sense of a community of learning, a larger proportion of faculty dedicated to teaching, more personal interaction between faculty and students, and more emphasis on education in an intellectual and moral/ethical context, few outsiders seem impressed. Some even question what these things mean. This book explores some of the strengths and weaknesses of the small college while offering some suggestions for maximizing the former and minimizing the latter.

"Bigger is better" as an American value may be of especially questionable relevance when applied to schools. Fond memories of the one-room school are not the only reason for resistance to consolidation of smaller neighborhood schools into the sometimes enormous and bureaucratized contemporary regional high school. In their classic study of high schools, Barker and Gump (1964) observe that when student benefits are the primary consideration, smaller is better. One of their main conclusions is that smaller schools have more student participation and involvement, important factors associated with achieving excellence in higher education (Astin, 1977, 1982, 1984a; National Institute of Education, 1984). It has often been observed that smaller schools produce a greater number of leaders in society in proportion to their size (see for example Barker and Gump, 1964; Martin, 1982). Of course, regardless of the size of the college or university, active and involved students have greater potential for future leadership, but the argument here is that smaller schools involve a greater *proportion* of their students. The number of participatory roles—in student government, play performance, debate, et cetera—is proportionately greater the smaller the school. *Barefoot in the Park* has a cast of six, whether it is performed at a college with 600 or 6,000 students. Shy young persons have more difficulty "hiding" in the small college—which can only benefit them later in life. Responsibility is less diluted.

SELECTIVITY IN ADMISSIONS STANDARDS

Selective admissions policy (rejecting many applicants) is another factor which brings visibility and prestige to larger, but not necessarily smaller, colleges. In the only comprehensive empirical study available on small colleges, Astin and Lee (1971:6) found that "highly selective institutions that have enrollments of under 500 are not widely known." Size is such an important factor in prestige formation that it strongly mitigates the impact of almost all other factors for the smallest schools.

It could be argued that high selectivity in admissions is a questionable policy for colleges in a society which portends to offer education, including higher education, to the masses of the people, but even if such a policy is desirable, few small colleges can afford to adopt highly selective admissions standards. For small colleges, a "Catch–22" situation emerges where small size results in low visibility, low visibility results in fewer applications, and fewer applications result in the relaxation of admissions standards. Ironically, however, as Astin and Lee (1971:82) note, selective admissions standards benefit neither the very small college nor the students typically served by them.

[W]ith respect to selectivity, the common belief that an elite or "high quality" institution provides a superior environment for learning is so far not supported by the evidence. . . . On the contrary, the cognitive skills of a student seem to develop at the same rate whatever the selectivity of the institution he attends. Thus contrary to popular opinion, the superior student is apparently no better off attending a highly selective institution; he would develop just as well intellectually if he attended a less selective one. . . . [O]ur traditional definitions of institutional "quality" may be inadequate or even erroneous.

IMPACT OF THE SMALL COLLEGE ON STUDENTS

As with other topics relating to small colleges, there are few data that deal with the impact of the small college educational experience on students. However, Astin's research (Astin and Panos, 1969; Astin and Lee, 1971; Astin, 1977, 1982, and 1984a) does directly and indirectly indicate certain educational benefits for small college students. For example, there is some empirical evidence that students tend to perceive the small college environment as warm and caring and larger colleges/

universities as cold and competitive (Astin and Lee, 1971:83). Astin and Panos (1969) found that attending a small college increases the student's chances of staying in school and eventually earning an advanced degree while attending a large institution has a negative impact on the student's desire to pursue graduate training and to get a Ph.D. Tucker (1984) extended the research of Hall (1984) which was a list of the top 100 private colleges and universities in the United States in terms of percentage of baccalaureate graduates who later earned doctoral degrees during the period 1920–1980. It was necessary for Tucker to supplement the listing to include small private colleges in Kansas that were ignored in the original study as being too small for consideration. Tucker found that in Kansas alone, twelve small private colleges achieved a doctoral productivity index which would have placed them in the range of the top 100 larger U.S. colleges and universities. Despite nonselective admissions standards, five of the small colleges actually exceeded the University of Kansas in the proportion of graduates who earned doctorates.

Well-equipped laboratories, professors doing high-level research, and the presence of graduate students are factors usually assumed to motivate students to pursue advanced, research-oriented degrees. In reality, these factors may be less important for motivating students than close faculty–student relationships, opportunities for student involvement and participation, and modest but accessible facilities. Here is where the small college can shine.

Of course, all is not perfect in Lilliput—there are certain unique problems associated with teaching in the small college. The purpose of the remaining chapters in this volume is to explore these problems and offer solutions.

CONTRIBUTIONS TO THE BOOK

In Chapter 2, James McReynolds describes some of the "terrors and triumphs" of teaching a full four-year curriculum in a one-person department. While McReynolds' comments are sometimes humorous, the chapter possesses much depth and offers numerous recommendations that would be beneficial even for larger departments in small colleges. Like other writers on college teaching (for example, see Eble, 1983), McReynolds emphasizes the inappropriateness of highly specialized, research-oriented graduate training as preparation for teaching and especially small college teaching.

In Chapter 3, Richard Wright examines what is perhaps the most common complaint of the small college faculty member—strain created by multiple and frequently conflicting roles and responsibilities. His analysis suggests some ways in which these strains can be used to the advantage of the small college professor.

Chapter 4 is a detailed description of a faculty development program implemented at Bellevue College in Nebraska. Author Joseph Wydeven provides an interesting guide for faculty development in the small college and concludes his chapter with a useful annotated bibliography.

In Chapter 5, David Smith strongly emphasizes the leadership role of the small college in the values/moral education movement. One danger in the small, church-affiliated college is that values education can become training in a particular religious orientation. Smith describes how to implement a values education program which is not inextricably bound to a particular set of values.

Robert Ward, in Chapter 6, "attempts to equip the reader to develop a computing facility well-suited to the needs of (the small campus) by sketching an appropriate procedural framework, identifying some of the major issues, warning about the most dangerous pitfalls and offering some generally applicable advice." This is a fairly detailed, step-by-step guide which does not ignore the human factors (often spelled p-o-l-i-t-i-c-s) involved in bringing computers to the small college.

Chapter 7 offers some tips on teaching courses outside one's areas of specialization—a frequent problem for the small college professor. With his tongue occasionally in-cheek, Richard Wright's "cookbook" approach will be particularly helpful to the beginning small college teacher.

In Chapter 8, Jan Vermeer tackles one of the thorniest and most debated issues in teaching in the small college—trying to balance a research agenda with heavy teaching loads. Vermeer notes that even in the small college, faculty are likely to gain as much or more recognition through research productivity as through teaching. Small college faculty interested in research will find many useful recommendations in Vermeer's chapter.

Richard Rempel (Chapter 9) states that "[e]stablishing cooperative departments among several colleges is one way to keep the advantages while ameliorating the disadvantages of small colleges." Hence, cooperative departments are an important solution to many of the liabilities to teaching in a small department mentioned by McReynolds in Chapter 2 and Wright in Chapter 7. Rempel's chapter describes a long-standing cooperative department in mathematics and computer sciences among several small colleges in central Kansas. A major benefit of the cooperative department is the exposure of the small college student to additional faculty who have different specialties and perspectives.

Physical education and coaching is the topic of Chapter 10. Paul Graber's discussion of the dilemmas encountered in balancing roles provides a good example of Wright's (Chapter 3) role strain in the small college. Graber contends the major university athletics model is not really workable in the small college.

Chapter 11 is a discussion of what it means for the small college to be both church-related and an institution of liberal learning. Donald Hatcher laments that "the task of 'liberally educating' students at church-related institutions is a tremendous challenge, one which I fear is all too often not adequately met." Still, he states the "opportunity for liberal learning may be unique to small church-related liberal arts colleges." The Hatcher and Smith chapters are complementary (also see Martin's *College of Character*, 1982).

One of the major problems of teaching in the small college is limited library holdings. This is more problematic for some fields than for others, but as Gregory Urwin (Chapter 12) indicates, the problem is especially acute for research in history. His solution: concentrate on local history research, using such resources as museums, newspaper files, local historical society collections, church files, and oral interviews. As Urwin states, an "enterprising student can unearth the traces of history almost anywhere."

Jeff Gundy (Chapter 13) concludes the volume with an informal, often humorous piece about one big university "sophisticate" who came to "fish in the small pond" of a small college. Gundy takes the reader from the ridiculous to the sublime in the small college intellectual journey. It is liberal education at its best.

Much awareness will be found in these pages of the problems associated with teaching in the small college; but there is celebration as well.

2

The Terrors and Triumphs of Teaching in a One-Person Department

JAMES K. McREYNOLDS

A college of 1,500 students or less can by all conventional standards be considered small, especially in comparison to major universities, which can have tens of thousands of students. In many small colleges there exists what some academicians might consider an anachronism in higher education reminiscent of the one-room school house—the one-person academic department. In these departments a single instructor is responsible for administration and virtually all the teaching. This creates unique demands, expectations, and limitations, which will be discussed in the balance of this chapter. (It should be noted that some of the problems mentioned below apply to departments consisting of up to four or five instructors.)

Having taught in such a one-person department for the last ten years, I find the experience analogous to riding a roller coaster. There are slow arduous climbs, frightening descents, sharp, unexpected twists, delightful heights, and dizzying sensations of speed. The one-person department is also like a roller coaster in that a short written account cannot adequately describe the experience. Still, to understand the operation of the small college it is essential to try to describe the trials and tribulations of the small department.

The following chapter is based on the observations, impressions, and views of the writer and colleagues in similar teaching situations. This approach is full of methodological weaknesses but still generates several potentially testable hypotheses. While objectivity is a laudable goal, it has been approached more than fully achieved in the discussion below. Also, while no two teaching environments are alike, I assume there are elements common to one-person departments in diverse situations, and hence some accurate generalizations can be made.

The academic demands of teaching in a one-person department are substantial. Faculty usually teach from nine to thirteen different courses every two or three years and three or four different courses per semester. To remain current with the advances within a discipline and to reflect this information in the classroom, considerable time must be spent in reading and preparing or updating lectures in many areas. Additionally, professors in one-person departments have administrative responsibilities and other institutional obligations to fulfill. This means that all departmental goals—budgets, course contents and requirements, textbook selections, test construction, grading, and academic advising are handled by one person who also serves on several institutional committees. Unlike the situation in large universities, there are no graduate and few work-study students to lighten the load. (While in some small colleges work-study students are available, the one-person department seems least likely to have access to them. This is because one-person departments are low in administrative priorities.) If a faculty member in a one-person department is a particularly effective teacher, class enrollments increase—which is greeted with joy by administrators, but also serves to increase the work load proportionately. Hence, the excellent instructor can literally become a victim of his or her success. The quality of support services provided for faculty varies widely—secretarial, copying, and printing services are excellent at some small colleges, but at others there may be a single student secretary who works part-time, spells poorly, and finds the handwriting of every faculty member illegible. There are the additional administrative encouragements to support the college's numerous extracurricular activities, to become active in community affairs, and if one has the time, to do research. Somewhere in this the faculty member is also expected to lead a personal life which serves as a model of American and/or Christian virtues.

If the reader had an image of teaching in a small college as one of general tranquillity, it should have evaporated by now. The small college may be located in a town which appears sleepy, on a sleepy-looking campus, but the only individuals who are genuinely sleepy are exhausted faculty members in one-person departments, particularly if they are new arrivals to teaching. There is invariably more work to be done than available time. It is not unusual for these faculty to find it almost impossible to leave their college professor role; they have no time for themselves and never feel free from the burden of work. Thus, the demands from one's academic discipline, the structure of the curriculum, the institution's expectations, and the desire for a meaningful personal life provide the basis for numerous conflicts within the instructor.

THE TERRORS

There appears to be no satisfying way in which a single individual can effectively accommodate the competing demands of the one-person department. The teacher knows what is expected in terms of an ideal performance, but confronts numerous constraints such as time, competing academic goals, other institutional responsibilities, and personal priorities. It can only be hoped that the teacher not only recognizes but also accepts the fact that there are substantial limitations to what can be accomplished. Compromises are made. Researching a "hot" area in the discipline may be indefinitely postponed. Previously used lectures are too frequently presented. Necessary reading is put off until the next vacation. Assigned textbooks are not completely read. Written student assignments are shortened. Tests become increasingly oriented toward objective questions. Attendance at college sponsored activities becomes curtailed. The instructor is constantly confronted with decisions regarding what must be done now and what can be postponed. In short, decisions are frequently made to do less than one's best. These decisions take a psychological toll. They are contrary to the instructor's professional training and to his or her personal expectations; yet, they enable the instructor to meet the daily demands of teaching. Still, these compromises leave the professor with feelings of inadequacy and guilt.

These problems can be illustrated by a tongue-in-cheek yet meaningful analogy from clinical psychology. Generally speaking there are three criteria used by psychologists and psychiatrists for determining severe mental disorder: degree of reality contact, level of social functioning, and the degree of danger posed to oneself or others (Seligman and Rosenhan, 1984). From a purposely exaggerated perspective the following is a description of how these criteria apply to teaching in a one-person department. (No suggestion is being made that the small college environment promotes more psychological difficulties than any other setting.)

The faculty member's reality contact is diminished by delusions of persecution by both students and administrators. Students seem to have devised a conspiracy which assumes the faculty member is available at least eighteen hours a day for whatever is deemed necessary—e.g., asking personal advice, killing time with idle chatter while waiting for another teacher they really want to see, borrowing valuable books which are inconsistently returned, questioning the nature of assignments, debating whether deadlines are absolute or relative, requesting recommendations, and asking to be excused from tests three days after the test was given. Feelings of paranoia are enhanced by administrators who reason that instructors who lecture just twelve to fourteen hours a week must have enormous amounts of time to spend sitting on committees, recruiting prospective students, and attending every college event even if it means being in two places at once. It is important for uninitiated readers to understand that small colleges sponsor an enormous number of activities over an academic year, including concerts, plays, guest speakers, athletic events, individual performances, group performances, admission days, field days, breakfasts, lunches, dinners, fund raisers, welcoming parties, farewell parties, birthday parties, swim parties, dances, movies, convocations, honorary doctorate hoodings, and still more athletic events. Feelings of persecution are enhanced by some students who seem to believe that the instructor's absence at "their" college event signifies personal rejection and by other students who note that the dean attends every event even if it really does mean being in two places at once.

Delusions about the administration are particularly evident in the weeks before contracts and departmental budgets are issued. "They" are going to terminate me because.... So-and-so is not going to be here next year because.... My meager departmental budget was cut because.... "They" do not think I support the college enough because....

Another aspect of diminished reality contact in the one-person department is the enormous amount of fantasizing engaged in by the instructor. The faculty member daydreams about classes filled with ideal students, what could have been better said (or would have been better left unsaid) in a previous class, delivering the perfect lecture, writing the seminal journal article, being able to get work done in one's office, getting every paper graded during the next vacation, all the wonderful things that will be done with the family over the summer, and finding a college which doesn't have all the problems of this one.

On a more serious note, reality contact is diminished in a one-person department by virtue of being alone. Without having same-discipline departmental colleagues, there is no one with whom to share ideas or to provide the feedback which is so vital to maintaining a current and balanced academic direction. Professional isolation can exacerbate feelings of inadequacy. Graduate training requires specialization within a particular area of the discipline. As such, the individual acquires a highly specific, yet limited expertise. The result is that graduate training may not have prepared the instructor new to a one-person department to teach several of the many courses required. In this terrifying situation, an immediate confrontation takes place with one's ignorance, and there is no one to provide help.

After teaching in a one-person department for several years, an opposite problem can emerge—the illusion that one knows everything within the discipline. This can produce deadly complacency, aloofness, stagnation, and pomposity, harming not only students and the college, but the instructor as well. Of the two problems mentioned—knowing too little and knowing too much—the consequences are ironically the same. In both instances the individual is isolated and ineffectual.

The problem of knowing too little is frequently exacerbated by three additional factors: distances, budgets, and library resources. The one-person department is most common in small colleges located in isolated geographical areas. The resources of a major college or university are usually at quite a distance, and because budgetary restrictions are common in small colleges, access to these resources is restricted. Budgetary considerations may also limit professional development to attending one or two regional conferences a year, and in some cases prevent sabbaticals. For faculty members who wish to attend professional meetings, personal finances must frequently be used to cover travel, lodging, and registration fees. On-campus budget restraints can also limit the number of available professional journals and monographs. Reading is the easiest and least expensive way to remain knowledgeable in one's field; yet, librarians can become quite recalcitrant in granting requests by claiming that too few students will make use of the materials. All the sources of isolation mentioned above cannot help but have a negative impact on the morale and effectiveness of a dedicated college teacher.

A second criterion by which mental disorder is usually identified is the individual's level of social functioning. This refers to one's ability to meet the general demands of daily living— of being able to maintain oneself in society. In applying this to the small college context it is relatively easy to succumb to exaggeration. Still, insomnia is not uncommon, particularly on Sunday nights with a week of incomplete preparations leering in one's face or on nights before and especially after examinations. Eating disorders are possible through eating too much to gain energy lost from overwork or eating too little because of having no time or losing track of time. Social functioning is also impaired by the guilt one feels by spending time with one's family as opposed to working; or by working and not spending enough time with one's family. Income level provides perhaps the largest impediment to social functioning—you know that you are in trouble when your graduating seniors accept their first jobs at salaries higher than yours, and you have been teaching for ten years. A first-time visitor to a small college might do well to observe the differences between the cars driven by students and faculty. New cars typically belong to students, and wrecks belong to faculty.

The final criterion for determining mental disorder refers to the degree of danger one poses to others or oneself. Faced with incredible demands, many faculty in one-person departments may wonder if they are committing slow suicide. Some of the symptoms reported include the inability to speak without a cup of coffee in hand, the appearance of a rut in the floor that runs directly from one's office to the pop machine, knowing where every ashtray in the entire college is located, and realizing that dining hall lunches with all the potato chips, breads, french fries, cakes, pasta, mystery meat, and grease provide the best meal in town for the money. As to the degree of danger posed to others, homicide looms as a possibility. Likely candidates include deans who coyly state that they have a favor to ask, students who call the morning before a scheduled test to request they be excused because their second cousin's nephew has tonsilitis, students claiming they were "sick" after they failed to submit an assignment on time, students who ask for test results thirty minutes after completing it, students who still misspell the instructor's name at the end of the semester, students who chew tobacco while you are lecturing, seniors who finally decide to apply to graduate school three weeks before commencement, bookstore managers who don't want you to change texts for a class because they have two leftover, nonreturnable copies of the old text in the storeroom, and presidents who arrive on campus driving a new college-provided car shortly after announcing departmental budget cuts.

In summary, the faculty member in the one-person department leads a complicated life that involves a series of seemingly unending, anxiety-inducing demands. Too often there is the feeling of being hounded, even haunted, by the spectre of things not done. While this situation is ideal for inducing a state of existential terror and despair, McGee's (1971) research reveals that small colleges also provide faculty members with genuine feelings of satisfaction and accomplishment. The demands and dilemmas of the one-person department offer many opportunities for professional fulfillment and personal growth. The small department provides considerable freedom and personal control, which can encourage exploration, experimentation, and innovation in teaching and professional development (see Sacks and Wiener, 1978). The remainder of the paper will suggest some ways for turning terrors into triumphs in the one person department.

CREATING TRIUMPHS

The most important factor in turning terror into triumph is one's attitude. As the first part of this paper illustrates, it is easy to consider oneself a victim of the teaching environment. However, there is also a strong element of reciprocity in this situation—the kinds of decisions the faculty member makes also change the nature of the environment, much more so than at a larger institution. The selection of textbooks, types and number of tests, form and content of written assignments, grading scales, and number and content of courses offered are largely a product of one-person's thinking. Once faculty in one person departments realize that they have considerable control over their working situation, effective and innovative decisions are possible. The triumphs in one-person departments emerge in three areas: (1) curricular construction and control, (2) institutional advantages, and (3) student development.

Curricular Construction and Control

The curriculum is not carved in stone—to think so leads to an element of stagnation or even the feeling of being trapped. Even though a core of courses may be required to give a basic introductory knowledge to a discipline and to meet graduate school admissions requirements, there is still room for some flexibility. At most small colleges curriculum is governed by a faculty committee whose members are familiar with the problem of maintaining a contemporary curricular structure with limited personnel and material resources. A major difficulty emerges when a new faculty member inherits a course structure reflecting his or her predecessor's biases and expertise. This, coupled with the constantly growing and changing knowledge within an academic area, the preferences of the new instructor, and the awareness of both institutional and personal limitations make most academic policy committees quite open to requests for change from one-person departments. However, an overzealous goal of attempting to duplicate the range of course offerings found in larger university departments can only work to the detriment of the faculty member and of the program.

To help compensate for a reduced number of course offerings, it is possible to construct courses with flexible contents which vary from semester to semester or special topics courses which change annually. These options enable the instructor to introduce, explore, discuss, and experiment with different content materials, methods of presentation, and student assignments.

Flexible curriculum and course content lend themselves to the small college because class enrollments are fairly limited and student feedback can be quickly elicited. For example, National Public Radio has available for purchase several thousand audio cassettes which are constantly being updated and expanded. An annually updated catalog of cassette offerings is available from most libraries or local public radio stations. These inexpensive cassettes frequently feature the leaders and major contemporary controversies found in many academic areas, making a variety of interesting issues and topics readily available for even the most modest departmental budget.

As another example, testing and lecturing can be virtually eliminated in upper-division classes by the instructor assigning several primary sources rather than the conventional textbook and having students submit a series of well-referenced response papers. The advantages to this approach are that students are directly exposed to the molders and shapers of the discipline and also develop and sharpen their own capacities for critical thinking. Student interpretations and reactions can then be incorporated into classroom presentations. This diminishes the need for traditional lectures, yet forces the instructor to be involved in the learning process in order to critique student interpretations of material. By adopting a role of the excited and active learner, the teacher thus presents a positive model of the personal satisfaction that can be derived through study. Students too rarely observe this in their teachers, which contributes to the perception that studying is onerous.

Working hard certainly is associated with competent teaching; however, it is possible to set personal expectations too high and work too hard. An excited, motivated teacher does more for effective learning than a tired, harried one. In teaching a larger-than-average load and a wide diversity of classes, there are enormous pressures on the instructor. Yet, the small college faculty member is no automaton; he or she needs rest, exercise, play, personal contacts, and an escape from work. A worthy goal is to construct a curriculum which encourages students to do more work while the instructor does less. As the above suggestions indicate, there are numerous ways this can be done without sacrificing academic quality or personal integrity.

Institutional Advantages

The small college experience offers a wonderful opportunity to feel a deep sense of community—that one is supportively and constructively involved in the life of the college. A professor can have a substantial impact not only in his or her department, but in the institution in general. It is possible for the instructor to see suggestions adopted regarding admission policies, general education courses, academic standards, and other institutional policies. There is much opportunity for the interests and abilities of the individual faculty member to be used outside one's discipline.

Another advantage for many small college faculty is the emphasis on teaching rather than research. Most small colleges actively avoid the "publish or perish" syndrome found at larger institutions. To a certain extent, the deemphasis on research is necessary owing to the teaching load and the number of different courses taught. However, the deemphasis on research is also chosen—most small colleges would lose their identity and mission were they to become research institutions. Perhaps it is heresy to suggest that publications are unnecessary to be an effective instructor on the undergraduate level. It has been suggested. One does not have to publish to become or remain a competent teacher, particularly given the constraints of the one-person department. Most administrators at small colleges appear to recognize this while many faculty members who are trained in the university model have some difficulty in doing so. This is partially an outcome of split allegiances—the administrator's loyalty is to the college while faculty members may feel more loyalty to their discipline. Small college faculty were typically indoctrinated regarding the importance of research publications while in graduate school, which can lead to the false perception of inadequacy or incompetence if publishing is not later pursued. Small colleges do benefit from the publication activities of faculty, but the generalist orientation of a one-person department makes it quite difficult to maintain or develop the necessary expertise needed for publication. A real source of triumph can be found in pursuing and realizing growth as a master teacher without the nagging anxieties which are sometimes associated with a lack of publications. This triumph can be accomplished by at least partially recognizing the inappropriateness of adopting a large university research model in a small college setting.

Student Development

Another source of triumph is contributing to and witnessing the overall growth and development of one's students. In the one-person department, the student and instructor can share up to four years of uninterrupted dialogue. The tentativeness of the first meeting can lead to a genuine friendship which lasts a lifetime. The teacher can see the memorization of basic concepts in the introductory course gradually transform into the reflective and critical thinking of a maturing scholar in upper-division classes. The personal growth of the students emerges through struggles with the material, their instructor, and with themselves, but with each struggle comes greater self-awareness and an increasing confidence in their abilities. Instructors in one-person departments are not just teaching, but also nurturing, supporting, and sharing with students. Students perceive that they are known as individuals—they are not "numbers," and their efforts generate genuine feedback. This is where the educational process at small colleges acquires distinction.

In one-person departments, the personal characteristics of the instructor are extremely important. Faculty in these departments quickly establish a campus-wide reputation as to knowledge, teaching ability, and interest in students. This reputation has an obvious impact on class enrollments and can sometimes mean the difference in the continuation of a marginal department. In the effort to hire the most qualified instructors, deans and search committees are naturally attracted to candidates with the strongest vitae. Hiring by vitae, however, may lead search committees to overlook candidates who have the necessary personal qualities to function effectively and enduringly in one-person departments. Again reflecting a divergence from the university model, the weight of a candidate's credentials should not overshadow the individual who possesses them. The type of person one is, particularly in responding to students, is far more important than what one has done. One essential personal characteristic for teaching in a one-person department is an appreciation of students. Such instructors resist dichotomizing student–teacher relationships as "us versus them" with the attendant forms of guerrilla warfare on both sides. Students need to feel a sense of personal worth even when (or especially when) they have failed.

Another essential personal characteristic is the instructor's willingness to maintain a program of academic integrity. This has two components—the willingness to establish demanding academic standards and an openness to a diversity of thinking within one's discipline. Especially in the one-person department, dogmatism is not the same thing as education. Rigid adherence to particular theories or concepts blinds students to the diversity that exists within all academic disciplines. To present material by emphasizing one view to the exclusion of others distorts the way that disciplines are constructed and operate. In the one-person department instructor dogmatism results in students unconsciously becoming disciples rather than developing their own critical capacities and substantiated conclusions. These students are apt to graduate with a major in their professor rather than in their discipline.

The willingness to maintain demanding academic standards and a genuine liking for students can be complementary. An effective instructor has high but achievable standards and is simultaneously willing to assist students in the quest for excellence. Students need to know they can improve academically and that the instructor is there cheering them on. With the knowledge that improvement is possible and the instructor is not an enemy but an ally in the learning process, the struggle can become one with the material and not with personalities.

In summary, the significance of the teacher's attitude and personality in the one-person department is hard to overestimate. It would seem, then, that in the hiring process the on-campus interview assumes critical significance. Assuming that the final list of applicants have all met minimum requirements, the personal characteristics of candidates are then vitally important. If this area is slighted, the opportunities for failure—and terror—experienced by the teacher, students, and administrators are multiplied. Ultimately, the administration must share some responsibility for the success or failure of a faculty member in the one-person department.

FINAL REFLECTIONS

As has been stated, the faculty member in the one-person department functions in a complex, diverse environment of professional obligations, institutional requirements, student demands, and personal limitations. This situation is unique in higher education in that it differs markedly from larger departments in larger institutions. In no other academic area is the instructor charged with such a broad range of responsibilities which must be met virtually alone. Therefore, some critics question the efficacy of having such programs at all. Even the university model of higher education, which has such great generalizability, has questionable applicability to the one-person department. Consequently, the difficulty of teaching in such a program is increased by having an inaccurate conceptual model which serves to cloud understanding and acceptance of such programs. This increases the faculty member's isolation both from his or her discipline and from academia in general. These issues led to the use of the word *terror* to describe the experience of teaching in a one-person department. Yet, as we have seen, terror can be transformed into triumph.

The existence of one-person departments is a continuing tradition in many small colleges. Yet the operation of these departments does not have to be traditional. Students should be provided with an appreciation for the richness of a discipline in terms of knowledge and a possible career. This can be achieved in many ways. Here, the isolation of the instructor can have advantages because although there is no one to provide feedback, there is also no one to prevent the implementation of plans. This opens the opportunity to explore and experiment with a variety of pedagogical techniques.

Teaching in the one-person department guarantees some constraints. While academic preparation, time, and resources are circumscribed, there are no limits on imagination. The environment may determine what the instructor can't do, but it doesn't tell him or her what can be done. May (1975) observes that limitations are a necessary ingredient for creativity. A willingness to question, a personal interest in one's students, and the inclusion of one's speculations and interests in teaching can produce a meaningful sense of challenge and excitement. Rogers (1983) writes that the personalizing of teaching generates profoundly positive consequences. When the instructor is excited about what is being taught, many more students become involved in the learning process than if a lecture is read from notes, or worse yet, from the textbook. Bad teaching is not determined by the environment in which it takes place, but by the decisions made by the instructor who is doing it. A one-person department by virtue of its small size does not imply mediocrity. As in all formal learning, the key factor is the quality of the teacher.

With the opportunities of a flexible program, teachers also have the occasion to use their abilities on a college-wide basis. Additionally, there is the very real likelihood of establishing academically constructive, personally meaningful relationships with students. The shared feeling of working together for a common goal adds an extremely rewarding psychological dimension to teaching. While there is no guaranteed immunity from the terrors of teaching in a one-person department, the faculty member can do much to lessen this possibility and to increase the probability of experiencing a sense of triumph.

3

Professorial Role Strains in the Small College: Issues and Opportunities

RICHARD A. WRIGHT

A frequent complaint of most small college personnel concerns the number of different "hats" worn relative to faculty or administrative positions—for example, administrators typically lament when they are called upon to teach while faculty likewise protest when they are called upon to administer. Sociologists explain such phenomena by referring to the concepts *status*, *role*, and *role strain* (see Linton, 1936; Merton, 1957; Goffman, 1961). *Statuses* are defined as the positions individuals occupy in a social structure. We all occupy numerous statuses such as husband/wife, mother/daughter, employer/employee, and teacher/student. *Roles* are defined as the behavioral expectations, obligations, and privileges associated with a status. The status of college student includes a variety of important roles such as attending class, taking notes, reading texts, taking examinations, and writing papers. *Role strain* emerges when either the role demands of a particular status cannot be met or the roles associated with a particular status exert conflicting demands. An example of the former is the divorced father who is unable to make child support payments; an example of the latter is the harried graduate student who devotes excessive time studying for one difficult course only to witness his or her grades slip in other courses.

This chapter examines role strains which relate to the status of teaching in the small college. All college faculty undoubtedly frequently experience role strains in their professorial status; yet, a major argument in this paper is that structural peculiarities in the small college exacerbate faculty role strains. I also offer a theoretical interpretation of two orientations that individuals often adopt in order to perform roles consistently and a recommendation for the constructive use of role strains in the small college.

ROLE PERFORMANCES AND ROLE STRAINS: A THEORETICAL OVERVIEW

Although a cursory interpretation might suggest that societies prescribe and enforce roles strictly and consistently, in reality considerable diversity is permitted and even encouraged in the performance of roles. Erikson (1976) observes that core cultural values and roles are arrayed on "axes of variation" which allow behavioral choices between socially prescribed "norms" and socially tolerated (if not prescribed) "counternorms." For example, while Americans highly value the core cultural role of the proverbial career-oriented "go-getter," this role can be performed on a socially prescribed "axis of variation" ranging from the norm of the "self-made man" to the counternorm of the "good team player." Merton (1976) uses the term *sociological ambivalence* to refer to the contradictory role performances which societies permit and frequently condone.

While societies encourage considerable variation in the performance of roles, individuals typically standardize interaction by gravitating toward role performance consistency. Thus the worker who achieves a reputation as a "self-made man" doesn't overnight become a "good team player." Indeed, persons who perform roles inconsistently often suffer from inner conflicts (Erikson, 1976) and run the risk of being stigmatized as eccentric or untrustworthy.

As Table 1 reveals, social scientists have traditionally argued that a fundamentally important axis of variation exists be-

Table 1
Some Theoretical Equivalents to "We" and "I" Orientations

Theorist(s) and Discipline	"We" Orientations	"I" Orientations
Ferdinand Toennies (Sociology)	Gemeinschaft	Gesellschaft
Charles Cooley (Sociology)	Primary groups	Secondary groups
Talcott Parsons (Sociology)	Expressive interaction	Instrumental interaction
Martin Buber (Philosophy)	I-Thou	I-It
Robert Redfield (Anthropology)	Folk societies	Urban societies
Robert Bales and Philip Slater (Social Psychology)	Socioemotional leadership	Task leadership
Murray Davis and Catherine Schmidt (Social Psychology)	Nice personalities	Obnoxious personalities

tween two contradictory personality orientations which structure and regularize all social interaction (see for example Toennies, [1887] 1957; Cooley, 1909; Buber [1923] 1970; Redfield,
1941 and 1947; Parsons, 1951; Bales and Slater, 1955; Davis
and Schmidt, 1977). Elsewhere I have used the terms "we" and
"I" orientations as shorthand references for the numerous social scientific concepts coined to refer to these contradictory

personality types (see Wright, 1976, 1984, and Table 1). Briefly, "we" orientations involve interaction which occurs as an end in itself (i.e., the interaction exists for its intrinsic satisfaction) while in "I" orientations, interaction is pursued to attain some reward or "end apart from the immediate interactive setting" (Wright, 1984:144). Examples of "we" orientations include play activity between a mother and her young child (here interaction is typically pursued for sheer enjoyment); an example of an "I" orientation is a customer's relationship with a supermarket cashier (here interaction is pursued to attain ends extraneous to the interaction—food for the customer and a wage for the cashier). Normally "we"-oriented role performances emerge in family interaction while "I"-oriented role performances flourish in occupational relationships. Failure to adopt the appropriate role orientation for the appropriate status or inconsistency in role performance contributes to role strain and renders interaction volatile (Wright, 1984).

THE SOURCES OF ROLE STRAINS IN THE SMALL COLLEGE

The socially prescribed roles for all college and university faculty contain some contradictory elements which result in role strain. Regardless of the size of a university or college, faculty members can be heard complaining about various onerous and time-consuming job requirements which they perceive are unrelated to teaching and research. The negative connotations attributed to such phrases as "publish or perish," "administraive paperwork," and "departmental politics" illustrate the universal features of at least two roles—publishing and administering—which contribute to role strain for most college faculty.

Still, two unique structural features of the small college compound the problem of professorial role strains. First, small college faculty are much less protected from the "real world" than their large university compatriots. A mathematician at a large university may teach in a department with as many as 75 colleagues. Large departments insulate the faculty member from interaction outside his or her discipline, enabling the professor to live, eat, and breathe one esoteric specialty. In contrast, organizational size compels the professor in the small college to participate in considerable interdisciplinary interaction (McGee, 1971). At small colleges, mathematicians may number biologists, historians, admissions counselors, and numerous local townspeople among their close friends. While most small college professors would probably contend that graduate faculty miss a great deal by not experiencing the cross-fertilization of ideas which emerges from extensive interdisciplinary contact, many small college faculty might also concede that interdisciplinary and intercommunity friendships and commitments frequently divide their time and loyalties. Lack of scholarly isolation and resultant faculty role strain means that the small college more closely approximates an ivory tent than an ivory tower.

A second and related feature which causes faculty role strain is "bare bones" staffing. The small college offers many of the same instructional and recreational programs as the large university but with far fewer personnel (producing the "multiple hats syndrome" mentioned earlier). In the small college, it is common to find a psychology professor who is also assistant dean of student services, an education professor who is a part-time institutional researcher, or a physics instructor who moonlights in the learning skills center. Too often, the multiple roles required of small college professors can cause them to become proverbial "Jacks of all trades who are masters of none."

ROLE STRAINS CONFRONTING SMALL COLLEGE FACULTY

Five major dichotomous role strains affect faculty in the small college:

1. Localistic versus cosmopolitan orientations
2. Teaching versus research commitments
3. "We" versus "I" relationships with students, other faculty, and staff
4. Generalized versus specialized career preparation for students
5. Faculty versus administrative responsibilities

Localistic Versus Cosmopolitan Orientations

Gouldner (1957) and McGee (1971) argue that college faculty can be classified as either "locals" or "cosmopolitans." "Locals" achieve need satisfaction through maintaining friendships and loyalties *inside* their particular institution while "cosmopolitans" look to professional disciplinary associates *outside* the institution for need satisfaction (McGee, 1971). Rich and Jolicoeur (1978) contend that most two-year college faculty have a localistic orientation while graduate faculty are more cosmopolitan-oriented. In contrast, McGee (1971:39) asserts that faculty in the small four-year college tend to be Janus-faced, with one face

turned inward toward the campus community and its members, concerned with the quality of life there and the enrichment of the social, psychic, and moral lives of those with whom it interacts...[and the other face] turned outward toward the wider arena of the world, responding to the standards imposed by professional allegiances.

Teaching Versus Research Commitments

Although professors in most American institutions of higher learning experience some strain between teaching versus researching roles, the problem reaches an extreme in the four-year college or university (McGee, 1971). While the reward structures of graduate universities and two-year colleges reduce this role strain by emphasizing the importance of research in the former and teaching in the latter, four-year colleges are caught mid-stream between these contrasting roles (McGee, 1971; Goldsmid and Wilson, 1980). Furthermore, Rich and Jolicoeur's (1978) study of California college professors reveals that teacher/researcher role strain is perhaps most pronounced in small four-year colleges. For example, 41 percent of Rich and Jolicoeur's small college respondents expressed an equal affinity for teaching and research while over 76 percent voiced interest in doing research despite heavy teaching loads.

Several scholars—most notably Goldsmid and Wilson (1980)

and Ratner (1981)—have recently proposed the "synergistic model" which emphasizes the complementarity of teaching and research (Baker and Zey-Ferrell, 1984). Proponents of the synergistic model contend that teacher/researcher role strain may be more illusory than real because both roles involve similar goals—the discovery and transmission of knowledge—and necessitate similar means to achieve these goals—organization, consummate preparation, and the effective use of time (see Goldsmid and Wilson, 1980; Friedrich and Michalak, 1983). Although there is little empirical evidence to indicate that active engagement in research actually improves student evaluations of teaching effectiveness (Friedrich and Michalak, 1983), Goldsmid and Wilson (1980:44) maintain that research involvement indirectly benefits teaching because "research fosters a command of current studies in a field and a sense of needed (empirical) tests and (theoretical) extension."

"We" Versus "I" Relationships with Students, Other Faculty, and Staff

Much role strain exists in the small college over the faculty member's choice of "we"- or "I"-oriented role relationships with students. While superficially the professor–student relationship might appear to be solely "I" oriented (the faculty member interacts with students to receive the extraneous "reward" of a salary while the student interacts with the faculty member to receive a good grade and ultimately a good job), frequent and prolonged faculty–student interaction can lead to the emergence of "we" relationships. A sudden reversal of orientations on the part of professors or students can lead to considerable interpersonal conflict (for example, when the "friendly" professor assigns a failing grade or when the "friendly" student becomes combative in the classroom). Over time, familiarity and proximity between small college faculty and students can create subtle norms which encourage grade inflation and discourage classroom debate as a means for preserving the comforting pretense of "we" relationships. Where professor–student "we" relationships predominate, however, academic rigor and scholarship may be sacrificed.

Role strains relating to "we" versus "I" orientations also affect faculty and staff interaction. Traditions, customs, and norms prescribe "we" relationships among small college personnel—an illustration is the tendency for administrators (especially in the presence of outsiders) to refer to the small college as "one big happy family." Practical structural constraints in the small college seem to require a "live and let live" ambiance—face-to-face interaction year in, year out with a small group of co-workers fosters a cosmetic ideology of cooperation and toleration. Yet tenure and promotion decisions require administrators and senior faculty to evaluate the performance of junior faculty—a phenomenon which suggests the hypocrisy of the "one big happy family" motif. In addition, grudges, status snubs, and grievances which date back for years and even decades sometimes fester just beneath the cooperative veneer of small college traditions.

Generalized Versus Specialized Career Preparation for Students

Sociological ambivalence emerges in many small four-year colleges because some faculty endorse a generalized, holistic approach to undergraduate education while others advocate career specialization and technical training. Faculty devoted to generalized career preparation typically believe that the ultimate goal of a liberal arts education is to "build character" while the appropriate means to this goal is a synthetic, holistic, interdisciplinary/interdepartmental curriculum (McGee, 1971; Eble, 1976). In contrast, faculty interested in specialized career preparation believe the ultimate goal of an undergraduate education should be to prepare students for a specific job (when the bachelor's degree is terminal) or graduate school (when a student desires to continue his or her education). Specialized career preparation forces students and faculty to adopt a narrow disciplinary/departmental focus, which permits little room for general education course requirements and electives. Freshmen are frequently caught in the middle of this disagreement—some of their professors reward eclectic and holistic thinking while others only reward the mastery of arcane skills. Many upperclassmen partially resolve this dilemma by adopting the perspective of their major professors—a phenomenon which unfortunately can perpetuate faculty role strain when these students enroll in classes outside their major. (Upperclassmen with a specialized orientation view general education and elective classes as a "waste of time" while their generalistic peers complain that specialized classes are "irrelevant.")

Faculty Versus Administrative Responsibilities

The "bare bones" staffing of most small colleges means that the professor must contend not only with crushing teaching loads but also with significant administrative responsibilities. For example, many small college faculty not only serve as full-time teachers but also as departmental and/or divisional chairs. Also, McGee (1971) notes that committee loads are staggering among small college professors. Although faculty who maintain heavy research commitments can always claim that research enriches their teaching by keeping them academically current and intellectually alert, it is problematic to suggest that committee loads similarly enrich teaching. In addition, small colleges seldom provide meaningful prestige and recognition for faculty who deign to participate in "institutional politics" (McGee, 1971). The profound contradiction between faculty and administrative responsibilities almost certainly makes this dichotomy the most vexing source of role strain in the small college.

PROFESSORIAL ROLE PERFORMANCE CHOICES: THE REAL AND THE IDEAL

As noted earlier, individuals usually avoid role strains by choosing to perform roles in a consistent, uniform, and stable fashion. This tendency has considerable relevance for small college professors chiefly because the five previously mentioned role strains are fairly consistently organized around "we" and "I" performances (see Table 2). In reality, most small college faculty probably resolve professorial role strains by selecting one "set" of performances (as summarized in Table 2) largely

Table 2
Consistent Role Performance Choices for Small College Faculty

"We" Role Performances	"I" Role Performances
1. Localistic orientation	1. Cosmopolitan orientation
2. Teaching commitment	2. Research commitment
3. "We" relationships with students, other faculty, and staff	3. "I" relationships with students, other faculty, and staff
4. Generalized career preparation for students	4. Specialized career preparation for students
5. Faculty responsibilities	5. Administrative responsibilities

to the exclusion of the other. Furthermore, there is sufficient flexibility in the structure of most small colleges so that a faculty member can thoroughly embrace either a "we" or "I" performance set without serious repercussions.

While undoubtedly making matters more comfortable, predictable, and manageable, the exclusive choice of one role performance set ultimately harms the small college professor's effectiveness as a teacher and scholar. An attempt toward synthesizing "we" and "I" role performances in a single professorial status is a much more challenging and productive—albeit time consuming—strategy. When describing "nice" and "obnoxious" personality types (which closely correspond to "we" and "I" orientations—see Table 1), Davis and Schmidt (1977) argue that "charismatics"—or individuals who blend the affability of the nice with the aggressiveness of the obnoxious—are the most socially successful personality types. "Charismatic" small college professors capitalize on role strains by situationally choosing when to adopt "we" and "I" role performances. The charismatic professor is interested in both local and cosmopolitan issues and relationships and strives toward excellence in teaching, research, and administrative responsibilities. Most importantly, the charismatic professor mixes caring with intellectual rigor when interacting with students—or to paraphrase Davis and Schmidt (1977), the charismatic ascertains what other people want and then pushes them in that direction.

Pursuing the charismatic role set requires the small college professor to master both ordinary skills (such as sociability, organization, and effective use of time) and extraordinary skills (such as disciplinary competence, empathy, and compassion). This peculiar combination of talents is lucidly summarized in a student description of a charismatic professor which I once overheard:

Dr. C takes us [her students] almost to the intellectual breaking point and then at the last minute before we explode, she'll take the time to have us over to her house for dinner.

Dr. C shrewdly comprehends how to take advantage of professorial role strains.

4

The Small College "Teaching Improvement Committee": A Case Study

JOSEPH J. WYDEVEN

The emphasis in the small college is obviously placed upon teaching—a profession, perhaps surprisingly, which few faculty know very much about. Most of us were educated to be "experts" in a specific discipline, with the tacit understanding that knowledge of content assured ability to teach it to others. As teaching assistants in graduate school, most of us were tossed haphazardly into the classroom teaching role with little preparation and even less supervision. Few of us had any specific courses geared to the profession of teaching. Although this ironic situation is now being addressed in graduate schools, it is nonetheless true that currently practicing college faculty have had little preparation for their primary responsibility—teaching well. What Gaff (1976:16) noted some years ago remains a serious problem today:

[T]he fact of the matter is that our colleges and universities are now staffed by faculty who, in general, have never studied the history of their profession, are unfamiliar with the topography of the educational landscape, are unaware of the professional literature in higher education, and have never been expected to formulate systematically their own philosophies of education or their views about teaching and learning. (See also Eble, 1976 and 1983; Ellner and Barnes, 1983)

This diagnosis is relevant to faculty at both universities and colleges, but because of heavy teaching loads and isolation from same-discipline colleagues, the situation may be exacerbated in the small college.

At Bellevue College—a four-year business administration, accounting, and liberal arts institution serving approximately 2,600 full- and part-time students with 34 full-time faculty and 50 adjuncts—we have come to Gaff's conclusions belatedly, but three years ago the faculty and administration implemented a program for faculty awareness, development, and self-help. This teaching-improvement program is centered in a faculty committee termed the "Excellence in Teaching Committee." This paper discusses the development of the committee and describes its various projects. As readers will see, in many respects our experiment is not without its ambiguities; consequently, the teaching improvement program is still undergoing significant changes.

The Excellence in Teaching Committee (henceforth referred to as the ETC) resulted from a widespread concern with the emphasis placed by the administration on a strenuous teacher evaluation process performed near the conclusion of every course. Our faculty understood what many academic observers have recently noted—the significant increase in "accountability." But as McKeachie (in Bess, 1982:11) observes:

Heavy emphasis on evaluation may serve to reduce poor teaching resulting from inadequate preparation and inattention to the responsibilities of teaching. However, it is also likely to result in less innovation, less emphasis on long-term outcomes of education, and most important, less enthusiasm and commitment of the kind of extraordinary time and effort characterizing individuals who enjoy teaching and who are wrapped up in the enjoyable complexities of determining the best methods for teaching a particular subject matter to a particular group of students.

Recognizing the need for faculty accountability, several full-time faculty believed that the college should make available an internal means for faculty support and teaching improvement. Through one of the five-year planning committees, a proposal was sent to administrators suggesting the initiation of a committee which would have the following specific goals:

1. To provide a faculty self-help and peer advisory center for discussion and improvement of instructional methods.
2. To establish a library of pedagogical materials specifically for faculty use.
3. To study the entire issue of effective evaluation of instruction, with the possible aim of establishing a system of rewarding excellence in teaching.

These goals seemed modest at the time, but as it turned out, the third goal ensnared us in problems with administrative procedures, so that we chose to modify and downgrade its importance.

In the spring of 1982, the president of the college opened discussions for such a committee; by midsummer the chair and the other members were selected, and preparations were made for the committee to begin operating at the opening of the academic year. The committee constituted four faculty members—selected from the areas of history, psychology, business administration, and English—along with the director of the Learning Center. Each of the faculty was given a one-course reduction and the chair a two-course reduction (based on a norm of nine courses per academic year). One of our first projects was to have ourselves videotaped in class, after which members of the committee met to critique classroom performances—a process which I recommend to anyone desiring a good dose of self-insight. In addition, we scanned the available bibliographies (e.g., Eble, 1976; Gaff, Festa, and Gaff, 1978; Lindquist et al., 1979) and read as much as we could on the goals and methods of implementing a teaching improvement program. We quickly discovered that the innovation we were pursuing already had a significant history as a "movement" throughout the nation (although centered in large universities). This recognition simultaneously encouraged and discouraged us. On one hand, we were forced to admit our previous ignorance of this material; on the other hand, we realized we would have significant information to help structure our program. (It must be noted, however, that despite the large amount of information available on teaching improvement, little specifically relates to teaching in the small liberal arts college.)

The immediate problem in September 1982 was to introduce the ETC formally to the faculty at large. From our initial reading we learned the necessity for caution. Gaff (1976:121) warns that a "precondition to reaching the faculty is to know how they perceive this new concept of professional development and the organization that implements it. Typically, faculty have a cautious, skeptical, or critical initial reaction." Lindquist et al. (1979) note that faculty may resist institutionalized teaching improvement programs because of fear of interference with their academic values and beliefs, suspicion of infringement upon their autonomy, anxiety about their teaching, skepticism about innovations, or ignorance of their own teaching problems. A teaching improvement program may constitute something of a threat; a typical faculty response is: "What's wrong with the way I'm currently teaching? What do these people think they can teach me?"

Our announcement of the formation of the ETC was met with precisely this mixture of skepticism and suspicion. One of the questions which emerged had to to with quantifying "excellence"—we were asked for statistical evidence pertaining to a definition of good teaching. We dodged this issue as irrelevent, because the underlying purpose of the committee was to deal with qualitative, not quantitative, concerns. Actual classroom experiences would be emphasized—e. g., the difficulties with certain teaching methods; the moments of doubt when we see our practices failing to work for their intended audience; the realization that we have overchallenged, underchallenged, or misunderstood students, or even the recognition that something which worked well could almost certainly be improved. Our personal, rather than statistical, approach may have been a mistake, because we were as a consequence perceived by some faculty as naive, by others as teachers who advocated trial-and-error techniques, and by still others as upstarts with little experience. That we *had* little experience we admitted, but we insisted our focus was on supporting faculty efforts, not on dictating the rights and wrongs of teaching.

We made a serious tactical error by appearing to be over-zealous in advocating the voluntary formation of TRIO groups—units of three faculty members alternating as performing teacher, facilitator, and commentator (see Bergquist and Phillips, 1975:230–33). In principle an excellent method for teachers to examine their classroom efforts in relatively nonthreatening ways, TRIO arrangements need to be introduced slowly. Our mistake was to pass around a sign-up sheet at the first faculty meeting of the new academic year, rather than waiting for a more propitious time after we had discussed the matter informally with key faculty. In this case, our belief in the TRIO principle blinded us to the need to establish faculty trust first (see Wolcowitz, 1982).

All things considered, suspicion was our chief problem. The ETC was perceived as a rather ambiguous branch of the administration, and the earnestness of our presentations did little to overcome the idea that somewhere in back of our idealism lurked the spectre of administrative control. Added to this was our own ambivalence concerning the issue of whether faculty should claim participation in ETC activities at the time of their annual evaluations. (In theory it seems fair to include such participation, but at the same time such inclusion borders closely on mandatory participation, thereby undermining the voluntary character of ETC activity.)

It would be pleasant to report that the first year of our activities—1982–83—was an astounding success, but that was hardly the case. It is true we "institutionalized" ourselves, and we were promised a separate room for meetings and the storage of library materials when the college library addition was completed the following year. Yet faculty response was disappointing. TRIOs which were begun appeared to disintegrate by midyear, and others never materialized, despite our belief that the concept was valuable. The faculty were extremely reluctant to have themselves videotaped in class, despite our assurance the tapes were theirs to keep. (There is an almost universal fear among instructors to having their performances video-taped. Self-knowledge of this sort may be useful, but it is also potentially embarrassing.)

Perhaps those who benefited most from the existence of the committee the first year were committee members themselves. The bimonthly meetings were nearly always interesting and sometimes resulted in debates about "traditional" versus in-novative teaching methods, lecture versus discussion ap-proaches, the implementation of audiovisual materials, and the differing pedagogical assumptions between "reflective" liberal arts and "skills training" orientations. These were important conversations—our discussions were producing significant in-sights into our teaching philosophies and assumptions.

Through most of the first year the committee felt the frus-tration of isolation. We doggedly read books and articles related to our teaching concerns and reviewed these in dispatches and in two ETC newsletters distributed to faculty and staff. There was rarely a response. But committee members were adjusting methods in the classroom and feeling an intense satisfaction, which we desperately wanted to communicate to others. Mean-while, the ETC Library grew to approximately 100 volumes—some culled from the general library collection and others se-lected by the committee (despite our requests that faculty sub-mit book orders to us, few did so the first year). We took heart that for some reason the administration felt we were doing something valuable; we were asked to submit requests for equipment to furnish the ETC Room, which would soon be available. We asked for and received our own videotaping equipment, a desk, filing cabinets, bookcases, and a conference table.

By the end of the year we realized that we needed to establish more trust among the faculty. During the summer of 1983, we shifted our focus from individual self-help activities to more communal academic concerns specifically linked to pedagogical aspects of faculty development. We began to see more possi-bilities for affecting the entire academic environment, while deemphasizing the more threatening activities having to do solely with the classroom.

Without infringing on the official professional growth program at Bellevue College, we attempted to link our efforts to the idea of holistic professional development. We found the rationale for the bridge between professional development (as it affects pedagogical concerns, not as it affects the content of various disciplines) and teaching improvement in the following statement:

Professional development has taken on new dimensions, a new depth and scope. The term no longer refers merely to activities that update and upgrade knowledge of a subject matter; professional development now incorporates more direct attempts to improve instruction, plan continuous career development, fashion mutually beneficial relationships with the institution, and even foster aspects of personal development. (Gaff, Festa, and Gaff, 1978:8; see also Bergquist and Phillips, 1975)

By adopting a professional development approach to improved teaching, we believed that we could increase our credibility and expand our potential impact.

The two most important program innovations of the second year were the inclusion of four workshops and two faculty seminars. Faculty attendance was mandatory only for the first workshop, held during the customary faculty seminar in the week preceding the opening of the academic year. The president of the college concurred with our desire to ask Professor Kenneth Eble to come to campus for one of those days. Professor Eble was, happily, an excellent choice to serve as our first speaker of the year. We wanted someone with a national reputation in teaching improvement, but someone who would also be stimulating in a low-key manner. Because Professor Eble came to us as a practicing teacher with many years of classroom and consulting experience, his observations about teaching were wide-ranging and general—he had no special axe to grind and no specific theoretical position or ideology to sell. His workshop was a success.

Of the three remaining workshops—all requested by faculty—two were devoted to concerns not directly related to the classroom. The first was a three-hour workshop on stress management; the second dealt with publishing in academic jour-

46 Joseph J. Wydeven

nals. By and large, both workshops were well received. But the final workshop was the most successful, intended to initiate discussions regarding the implementation of a "Writing in All Disciplines" program at the college. This workshop dealt with a concern expressed by most academics these days—the apparent decrease in student ability to write competent prose. The session was led by two faculty from the University of Nebraska who had experience in working with faculty perceptions of writing, and they put us to work writing and sharing our results with others. Thanks to their tact and exuberance, the session went well, and many of those who attended spoke later of changing their future syllabi to accommodate what they had learned. (It is interesting to note that some of those faculty who most frequently complain about poor student writing and find the composition faculty remiss in their responsibilities were conspicuously absent.)

The second innovation—two faculty seminars referred to as the ETC Forum—was initiated to promote interdisciplinary intellectual exchanges among faculty members. The specific objectives of the forum were to institute planned faculty discussions on a formal basis (using a seminar method) and to increase faculty unity and morale. At the very least, those who attended the forums could be expected to come together over a chosen book and to share their perceptions with other colleagues. Conducted in a civilized and tolerant manner, the forum as an "institution" was intended to enhance the general level of faculty discourse—changing discussions about wayward students, the follies of the administration, and scuttlebutt about who is doing what in whatever strange corner to more enlightened concerns.

During the summer, we decided on three basic criteria for the selection of forum texts:

1. Books selected must be interdisciplinary without being overly technical.

2. Books must be controversial.

3. Books must have potential to affect the values of students in all classes in the curriculum.

This last point remains somewhat ambiguous, but what we meant was that books would be chosen on the basis of their potential to filter down to students in any discipline. More important, the ideas in books should aid students in questioning the purpose of their education in general. In short, the books chosen should "widen cultural horizons." The administration agreed to support the forum sessions by purchasing book copies for faculty and staff who intended to participate, as well as by providing refreshments.

As the topic for the first forum we chose Joseph Wood Krutch's *The Modern Temper* (1929). About 25 people participated in the session, enough so that we decided to split into two groups. Four participants wrote response papers of four to eight pages intended to initiate discussion.

The comments afterward from participants were generally reassuring. It was particularly gratifying to hear one respected member of the faculty claim that the Forum was "the best thing the ETC has done since its beginning." We took comments like these as indicators that the forum was academically sound. Afterwards the committee met for purposes of evaluation and decided that on the whole it was a qualified success. We were somewhat chagrinned that some faculty who had received books had not shown up, but given the pressure on faculty time, this seemed quite excusable as long as the administrators agreed with our perhaps cavalier attitude. We believed that the forum was worth doing again.

Accordingly we cast about for a book for the second ETC Forum to take place in April, and we finally agreed upon *1984 Revisited* (1983), a collection of essays, edited by Irving Howe, responding to George Orwell's novel. One assumption we made was that most faculty had read Orwell's novel, or knew enough about it to be able to make sense of the essays in the Howe collection; this seemed a valid assumption given the television, radio, and conference time recently devoted to *1984* (and given the fact the English Club had devoted New Year's Eve to a ten-hour public reading of the novel to which faculty and staff had been invited).

This forum was not as well attended as the first—I suspect for the very good reason that faculty were weary as they came to the end of another long year of teaching. No one, including members of the ETC, found time to write seminar response papers, and we had to settle for three or four one- or two-page summary statements to start the discussion. The group quickly polarized into two positions: One party argued that there are distinct totalitarian influences in American culture, while the other party assiduously denied the assertion. Yet despite the polarization of attitudes, we were forced to explain ourselves— and I think the result was a closer understanding of *why* others can hold opinions so contrary to our own. Certainly, this understanding is a value which we should pass on to our students, and I believe it is a value which faculty themselves ought to take more seriously. Insofar as the faculty gained insight into their own assumptions, the second forum was a success.

The ETC Forum is quite likely to be repeated in the coming year, though it seems important to bear in mind that faculty members may not have sufficient time to read entire books, especially toward the end of the academic year. Particularly for the April forum, it may be wiser to focus on an article or an essay, something short enough to read in one sitting and relatively easy to respond to. By reducing the amount read, it may be possible to include more participants. One might, for example, anticipate lively discussions developing from an essay on faculty motivation found in *The Chronicle of Higher Education* or a journal dedicated to teaching methodology.

A second point to be considered is the importance of including as many faculty interests as possible. Books or articles should be chosen which have appeal to social scientists as well as to those in business; to teachers of chemistry, mathematics, or physics as well as to those in the humanities. This task is not easy, but obviously the more immediate relevance the faculty perceive, the larger the participation may be. Two books currently being considered for next year are *In Search of Excellence* (Peters and Waterman, 1982) and *Megatrends* (Naisbitt, 1982).

In addition to these new programs, the ETC continued to develop projects from the preceding year. Perhaps the most significant progress was made in the growth of the ETC Library—due in large part to generous funding made possible by the college library expansion (as part of which the faculty were encouraged to order books). Some faculty who had not previously ordered through the ETC Library now began to request books specifically related to the pedagogy of their own disciplines. By the end of the 1983–84 academic year, the ETC Library had grown to over 200 volumes, so that it became necessary to shelve them under separate headings. Whereas in the first year we emphasized acquisitions dealing with teaching improvement and the philosophy of the teaching improvement "movement," in the second year we branched out into books on pedagogical theory (e.g., Bloom et al.'s *Taxonomy of Educational Objectives*, 1956); resources on specific skills such as the employment of group discussions and problem-solving exercises; books devoted to the behavior of students, administrators, and professors; materials on problems in writing and how to solve them; and "how-to" books on asking better test questions, on the implementation of audiovisuals and computers, and on designing innovative approaches. In addition, we ordered subscriptions to some of the important journals devoted to teaching: *Educational Theory, Harvard Educational Review, Improving College and University Teaching, Liberal Education, Research in Higher Education,* and *New Directions in Teaching and Learning.* Unfortunately, our efforts to encourage faculty to submit copies of their publications, theses, and dissertations met with little success.

We continued the ETC Newsletter in the same format as the preceding year, with reviews of exceptional books or articles, commentary, announcements, and a guest column (for which we persuaded a non-ETC member to submit ideas relevant to teaching). Our attempts to get an exchange of ideas going in this format have largely failed, and it is likely we will discontinue the newsletter in the future. The same purpose may be served by disseminating information in a memorandum format and through announcements at monthly faculty meetings. The newsletter, though a good idea in theory, may be unnecessary on the small campus where information often spreads by word of mouth.

We were also not particularly successful in our formal attempts to encourage individual faculty to discuss teaching problems, although many faculty shared experiences infor-

mally with individual members of the committee. Little official
videotaping of classroom performances was done, and the TRIO-
model peer groups were not formed along "official" lines. It
seems that the committee has had a greater impact in an informal way than through structured programs geared to get
individuals to seek assistance. There may be many reasons for
this: perceived lack of time, embarrassment, lack of trust in
committee members, laziness, complacency due to "passing"
student evaluations, or worse yet, lack of real interest in or
concern with the teaching role.

We begin ETC's third year with some trepidation and considerable ambiguity. Reviewing the progress made in the last
two years, we wonder precisely what our role should be. That
the committee has advanced the interests of the college is clear;
that it has had significant impact on the profession of teaching
at Bellevue College is less clear, although the committee members themselves have benefited greatly. If in the first year we
were too assiduous in attempting to get faculty involved, in
the second year we stepped back and emphasized programs
conducive to affecting the entire college environment. The suc-
cesses of the second year are clearly more apparent than those
of the first.

Since the inception of the ETC, the administration has desired quantifiable data and documented evidence that the committee has been effective in its primary goal of improving
instruction. Quantifiable evidence, however, is difficult to produce, especially considering that we have agreed upon ano-
nymity of faculty participation. At the time of this writing, the
ETC has been asked by the administration for a clear statement
of its operating principles and its rationale for existence prior
to further funding. As chair of the ETC my response is that
much of our impact is "invisible." We have overcome some of
the suspicion attached to us in the beginning, and the workshops and forums were fairly well attended. It would, of course,
be useful to know how workshops have changed faculty methods of teaching, but this is difficult to know given the conditions
of relative faculty autonomy (see Ellner, 1983).

My "philosophy" for the ETC is twofold: on one hand, we are
interested in teaching improvement—those things which go

into making the classroom performance better, more interesting, and more rewarding for students and faculty alike. On the other hand, we have become more interested and involved with "intrinsic motivation" (see Bess, 1982) and the impact of the academic environment on the minds of those men and women who profess teaching in particular disciplines (this concern has less to do with teaching per se and more with the human needs of individuals). In short, I believe the aims of a professional development program should go hand-in-hand with the objectives of teaching improvement.

It seems likely that the ETC will continue in the future, but the emphasis will be placed more actively on affecting the classroom itself. What form this will take is not yet clear, but I expect we will be asked to renew our efforts to have faculty videotaped, to oversee TRIOs, and to encourage workable innovations, in addition to working much more closely with adjunct faculty. Even assuming the worst—that the committee would cease to function—we have a great deal to show for our activities to this point. Several faculty have become convinced that teaching improvement *ought* to be a priority, and improvement in pedagogical methodology is now seen as a legitimate part of professional development. The accumulated library materials will remain—and because many of these books would have otherwise not been ordered, this is an important contribution to the resources of the college.

But I believe the ETC will continue to exist because it performs a vital function. The administration has supported us generously in the past because it has perceived that this is one of those rare phenomena which the faculty—at least a part of it—has itself requested and pursued. This is the only organization on campus which is devoted exclusively to the welfare of the faculty *as teachers*. Why, indeed, might administrators want such a program to come into existence and continue? The fact is that when a body of faculty is cognizant of the needs of students, is dedicated to the task of teaching (perhaps more than to the joys of pure scholarship), and is interested in the welfare of the total institution, the entire college benefits. Small colleges often have a high turnover of faculty, so there is sometimes a lapse in academic continuity, a problem which a teaching committee might help assuage. On the other hand, in cases where small departments are stable, fresh blood rarely enters from outside. Thus it is imperative that faculty with long tenure renew themselves from within. Obviously, administrators have a stake in programs which can stimulate reinvigoration and cut down on the stagnation which threatens when new ideas are rejected (and the same set of notes used, the same attitudes toward teaching expressed, year after year). To the degree to which an institution is financially healthy, administrators should be expected to support teaching improvement programs with at least minimal funding.

* * *

If . . . the [academic] setting is a conservative one in which heavy teaching loads and pressures to publish allow little time for improvement, in which there is little trust between and among faculty and administration, in which students and faculty have very little in common, and in which there is almost nothing in the way of expert assistance for the professor who seeks to improve teaching, it will take a magnifying glass to find much teaching improvement. (Lindquist et al., 1979: 40)

Although Lindquist et al.'s quotation summarizes many of the problems which threaten a teaching improvement program, there are three other difficulties I would like to discuss. First, there is the problem of deciding what the program will do to promote teaching improvement. Our experience indicates that there are two major paths to the goal of teaching improvement—the first is to effect changes in individual faculty members (in which case the program may be viewed suspiciously as "remedial"); the second is to work toward attempts to increase intrinsic motivation through holistic environmental change. In the second case proof of impact is difficult to adduce. (See Bergquist and Phillips, 1975, who discuss three approaches to faculty development through instructional, organizational, and personal development.)

The second problem—funding—is a ticklish issue in many institutions in the 1980s and inevitably involves faculty-administration relationships. It is difficult to believe that an effective teaching improvement program can be implemented without close and understanding cooperation between administrators and faculty. Fortunately, such programs need not require extravagant funding, and there are several directions to which one might turn: for instance, funding may already be available for traditional faculty development, and some of this might be channeled toward teaching improvement. It is conceivable that funds may be available through state or local resources in the form of grants to education. Reduced teaching loads for a semester or a year are extremely good motivators for faculty most interested in establishing a program; an alternative is the creation of an exploratory task force whose members might be released from other committee and administrative responsibilities.

Most campuses, no matter how small, have a room which is unused or which could be converted into a center for faculty improvement; conversion of a section of the faculty lounge (for those campuses with such a luxury) into a teaching improvement area is another way to enhance the "official" status of the program. Even though books will need to be ordered, there is no need for specialized storage; a section of the library could be reserved for pedagogical interests, with a list of resources maintained by the librarian. Book ordering need not be expensive; a portion of the current library budget might be allocated to faculty involved in teaching improvement.

A third issue wise to address is the nature of the faculty. Are they interested in improvement, or can they be persuaded to become interested? Are they open to the reasonable discussions of new ideas? Are they aware of the means that human beings use to project fears and inadequacies? In general, faculties may be classified into three basic types in relation to teaching improvement. There are key faculty who may be relied on for support and enthusiasm; there are "neutrals" who are willing to get involved if they can be convinced the value of involvement compensates for the work expended; and finally there are cynics who customarily put up resistance to any new idea. Fortunately, the latter are few, for personal pride often forbids open admission of inflexibility. It is unlikely that a teaching improvement program will reach the cynics, but it may have the potential to persuade the neutrals.

Although faculty and administrative cooperation is essential, there may be difficulty persuading both groups that a teaching improvement program is necessary or useful. Here, reading is helpful, because the literature on teaching improvement is quite persuasive. I recommend three fundamental texts:

1. *Designing Teaching Improvement* (Lindquist et al., 1979). This book contains vital information dealing with the rationale for implementing a program; how relationships among students, faculty, and administrators affect program implementation; liberal arts and community colleges; various teaching improvement programs in existence at the time of writing; and an extremely useful bibliography and project list with names and addresses of people to contact for further information. Lindquist et al. (1979:253–54) argue that teaching improvement programs should have three purposes: meeting "the learning needs of each student"; assisting "in the personal and professional development of each staff member"; and facilitating "the continuous development of institutional conditions which encourage and reward teaching improvement."

2. *Professional Development: A Guide to Resources* (Gaff, Festa, and Gaff, 1978). This book is divided into eleven chapters dealing with faculty development, including sections on "Faculty and Teaching," "Course Development," "Faculty Evaluation," and "Institutional Change." The virtue of this book is succinctness—each chapter begins with a brief discussion outlining the specific topic, followed by an annotated bibliography of recommended sources.

3. *A Handbook for Faculty Development*, Volumes 1–3 (Bergquist and Phillips, 1975, 1977, and 1981). The first volume includes essential information for implementing a teaching improvement program; the other two volumes add experiential information. The emphasis here is on practicality, and the books include exercises and models for workshops and the development of specific teaching skills.

With these books in hand, perhaps the next thing to do is contact relevant programs and publishers. Most centers which publish newsletters will send out copies and add names to their mailing lists. One extremely important publisher of books and other materials on teaching improvement is Jossey-Bass (433 California Street, San Francisco, California, 94104). An association dedicated to the well-being of teacher improvement efforts is the Professional and Organizational Network in Higher Education (contact Dr. Michelle S. Fisher, Center for Teaching and Learning, Stanford University, Stanford, California 94305). I also recommend visits to colleges with established programs in order to think through what modifications might be needed to implement the program in one's own institution.

Finally, if all else fails, individual faculty members may need to fall back on their own resources to stimulate more creative teaching. In this situation, several other books are invaluable. For purposes of getting started in the literature of teaching improvement, Kenneth Eble's *The Craft of Teaching* (1976) and *The Aims of College Teaching* (1983) are useful. Both books offer practical advice and probe the philosophical assumptions of higher education. Eble's views are sometimes controversial but always stimulating. Two practical books for beginning college teachers are Wilbert McKeachie's *Teaching Tips* (1978) and Margaret Gullette's *The Art and Craft for Teaching* (1982).

Perhaps the best single book conducive to the self-examination of teaching style is Fuhrmann and Grasha's *A Practical Handbook for College Teachers* (1983). Fuhrmann and Grasha combine hard data on teaching with self-help exercises without being dogmatic or prescriptive. The authors present information and exercises on cognitive, behaviorist, and humanistic perspectives on learning; they also include chapters on student learning styles and motivation, the use of media, evaluation, and innovations in course design. I particularly recommend Chapter 2, "The Role of Personal Values in Teaching," for helping faculty to comprehend and incorporate their values in course designs and teaching methods. The book concludes with a chapter entitled "Toward a Definition of Effective Teaching," which helps faculty to examine their teaching methods in relationship to the suggestions encountered earlier in the book.

There are, of course, scores of other interesting and useful books, and the reader will often find good ideas in unexpected places. The point is to begin somewhere and to find those unexpected places. The excitement created by these discoveries has the potential to be contagious. If enough "key" faculty become enthusiastic anew about teaching, the seed may be present for a concerted effort to affect the teaching environment throughout the college.

One final word: Teacher improvement programs will be most effective under two important conditions. The first is that the faculty must be convinced that teaching improvement is desirable; the second is that the faculty must be given sufficient time to make teaching improvement a reality. Both conditions are problematic in many small colleges, and to the degree they are insufficiently addressed or understood by faculty and administrators, improvement programs will be jeopardized. Faculty and administrators who expect immediate improvements in student evaluations may be disappointed. Further, faculty who already receive "acceptable" evaluations will probably have little initiative to try anything new, for fear of tinkering with what has worked in the past. Yet most good teachers know the intrinsic pleasures in teaching which provide motivation for care and improvement. It is the function of a good teaching improvement program to increase these intrinsic pleasures and thus to increase the quality of teaching in the institution as a whole.

5

Values Education

DAVID C. SMITH

In the last decade the higher education community has demonstrated a renewed concern for teaching about values. A recent article in the *Chronicle of Higher Education* reported on new values-oriented programs at nineteen institutions (O'Brien, 1976:5). The Association of American Colleges' *Forum for Liberal Education* devoted a 1982 issue to "Teaching About Values and Ethics" with reviews of the initiatives of more than a dozen schools. Scores of colleges have introduced courses on science and values and the number of courses in ethics at the undergraduate and professional school level is estimated at 11,000 (Hastings Center, 1980:5). Importantly, major new works on the teaching of ethics and values inform the discussions and curricular planning at many institutions (Morrill, 1978; Sloan, 1980; Chickering, 1981). As enthusiasm for the teaching of values grows in virtually every quarter of higher education, teachers and administrators at many small colleges may well entertain feelings of satisfaction. After all, values development has been an explicit goal of many small colleges since their founding. Indeed, isn't the primary virtue of a *small* institution its potential for creating community, for developing personal acquaintance between students and teachers and providing both with support as they question, refine, and live out value commitments? Wasn't the "value-free" scholarship, now under attack, the heritage of a university model that remained alien to the small college? As large universities are now being criticized for turning out specialists who remain egocentric moral infants, can't smaller colleges smugly maintain that they have been doing the right thing all along?

I believe that effective values teaching does require capabilities that have been traditional strengths of small colleges and that these institutions have exceptional opportunities to respond to the new demands for values education. However, a closer consideration of some of the current issues tends to dispel any complacency about relying on past success.

Small colleges—even those with strong religious roots and church ties—cannot escape the problem of deciding *which* values and patterns of values they should attempt to affirm, critique, clarify, or inculcate in the curriculum. In many cases a strong agreement exists about a core of basic values, but as institutional missions, personnel, and student populations shift, long-standing assumptions need to be examined in steady and careful institutional dialogue.

Beyond the question of which values we should teach, there is another set of current issues regarding curricular organization. Should an explicit concern for values be expressed through courses on values, or do values issues arise adequately in many courses structured along traditional, disciplinary/departmental lines? Over against the view that any solid liberal arts education will deal satisfactorily, if implicitly, with values, there are calls today for specific courses and units on values at the undergraduate level.

A third set of new issues relates to the pedagogy of teaching values. New insights about intellectual and moral development are widespread topics of discussion, but the assessment of the implications of these theories for classroom teaching is just beginning.

In sum, developments deserving the attention of faculty members and administrators at small colleges are occurring in three broad areas: value priorities, curricular organization, and pedagogy. The remainder of this paper examines these areas in detail.

WHAT VALUES CONCERN US?

As academic leaders reflect upon the question of which substantive and procedural values need to be stressed today, many begin by asking which values seem most threatened within our institutions and the wider society. Frequently, educators place *community, honesty, respect for others,* and *compassion* high on the list of endangered value species. This list emerges again and again in discussions within the Society for Values in Higher Education, and I shall refer to these as the "critical" values.

The threat to these critical values appears to be a growing ethos of individualistic self-interest, untempered by a sensitivity to the needs and rights of others. This is not the place to review the various historical-cultural hypotheses that would attempt to account for such a development. I would merely observe that both the causes and the prospective remedies may be very complex and subtle. As we seek constructive solutions to a perceived problem, it is important to avoid oversimplifications.

One oversimplification is to regard the problem of threatened values as simply the result of changing student attitudes. To be sure, there is good reason for concern about the trends in attitudes discovered by Astin (1984b) in his annual surveys of the views of almost 200,000 college freshman. Since 1966, when the survey was first conducted, the percentage of respondents who consider important or very important the value of "being well-off financially" has climbed from 40 percent to 70 percent, while the percentage who consider "developing a meaningful philosophy of life" important or very important has declined from over 80 percent to under 50 percent. In the late 1960s the goal of developing a meaningful philosophy of life ranked highest among the score of options presented as possible objectives for attending college and the second most frequently selected goal was "learning to get along with other people." Today, by contrast, "developing a specialty" ranks first, with "becoming very well-off financially" second.

The outlook of today's incoming students does hold challenges for anyone who shares my view that the goal of values education is to assist a person in an engaged effort to define and articulate a coherent view of the world that can be the basis for action in the service of humanity. Insofar as the attitudes of incoming students suggest a decreasing concern for interconnection and an increasing obsession with fragmenting specialization, we are up against tough problems.

Yet, the threat to the critical values is not only external, or something having to do with different generations of students. More to the point—and more as the starting point for change— we must recognize the threats to the values of community, honesty, respect, and compassion that arise within our own institutions, especially under circumstances of adversity. Conflicts between faculty and administration, lack of communication, academic specialization that depreciates the unity of knowledge are all threats to the critical values that come from ourselves. At the risk of stating the obvious, there is a close connection between the ability of colleges to sustain the critical values in their own institutional lives and their capacity to affect student values development. There is little chance of advancing the values of honesty, intellectual rigor, compassion and community if these seem absent in the life and practices of the college. Yet it is precisely these values that seem to be at risk. With faculty morale often low, competition for institutional resources increasing, and a management outlook colliding with collegial decision-making, the mission of values education can be thwarted unless communication, dialogue, and devotion to the institution go beyond self-interest. Conversely, when the institutional ethos embodies the critical values, there is a *real context* for values education. It is not easy to "change" something as subtle and pervasive as the ethos of an institution, but a renewed commitment to values education might energize many other aspects of institutional life. Insofar as citizens of the community of inquiry relate to each other honestly, respectfully, and compassionately, the potential for nurturing the development of these values among students is present. Even so, many questions of strategy and intention remain with regard to the "teaching" of values.

VALUES COURSES?

Significant questions about human purpose and meaning arise in the serious study of any discipline. Liberal arts education is potentially value-laden in ways that transcend its diverse forms of organization. Why then is there such frequent discussion of organizational issues, specifically, of introducing special courses on values?

Here again there are several considerations behind the question. Perhaps the foremost problem is whether a solid liberal arts education is automatically a values-oriented education. At most colleges, the curriculum is organized around the disciplinary major. Some faculty members may subtly (or not so subtly) convey to students the notion that core or distribution requirements are something to get out of the way in preparation for what really counts. At this point the professional self-interest of the faculty and the vocational self-interest of the students can coincide to produce a curricular ethos of specialization. Specialization—with all its inevitability in the face of the growth of knowledge and all of its advantages for producing further knowledge—can also lead to a neglect of broad and profound questions of human meaning or the dismissal of these questions as a problem for some other specialist. Specialization can easily lead to *fragmentation* of knowledge in which values issues—complex and ambiguous as they are—fall through the cracks. The Society for Values in Higher Education has sought to address this problem by creating ongoing cross- and interdisciplinary discussion groups and colloquia and establishing postdoctoral programs to support scholars attempting to relate developments in different fields.

Small colleges have strengths that may help to counter the problems of fragmentation, but there is little hope of avoiding the difficulty altogether. Small size may encourage (or force) faculty members in different fields into committee, social, and sometimes intellectual contact. Limited faculty size may preclude the design of courses that are extremely specialized. Yet,

as long as the graduate education of incoming faculty is an
exercise in specialization and the reward systems of higher
education are based upon disciplinary scholarship, small colleges are scarcely immune from the academic pressures that
sometimes allow a concern for values to slip away. The problem
is compounded by the fact that some faculty members as well
as students may regard the values issues that arise in their
studies as soft and elusive matters, as opposed to hard, factual
knowledge. And even where the disposition to engage in exploration of values issues is present, there can be what Langerak (1982) calls a "laudatory reticence" against holding forth
in an area where enthusiasm often outruns competence. Speaking about ethics, Langerak (1982:2–4) observes that:

> most natural scientists, many social scientists and even many instruc-
> tors in the arts and humanities feel unable to teach responsibly about
> ethical issues, fearing that they will either indoctrinate students on
> the basis of their own feelings or simply sow more confusion.

As a way to address this sentiment, he recommends that colleges provide adequate support for the development of team-
taught courses involving ethicists and scholars in other
disciplines.

Before examining another important source of the call for
courses on values, a particular word about the humanities and
values is in order, for it would seem that studies in these disciplines, however organized, impose serious reflection on values. Why can't we rely upon the humanities distribution
requirement to meet our responsibility for values education?

Unfortunately, disciplinary scholarship in the humanities
has become as specialized and fragmented as that in the social
and natural sciences and has the same potential for losing sight
of the values nexus of culture by concentrating on the study of
a few isolated artifacts or texts. Sophisticated methodologies
in philosophy, literary studies, and history oppose naive attempts to find easy lessons in texts and events. Insofar as these
methodologies challenge the assumption that we can get at the
intent of authors, the traditional locus for raising values questions is lost. I do not wish to dwell upon the problem of how to

encourage normative inquiry in the study of literature, philosophy, and history, except to observe that the moral relevance of these disciplines requires a careful, not a naive, defense.

To return to the general question of the teaching of values and the organization of the curriculum, the value of coherence invites a brief consideration. Is our hope for values education satisfied when this or that values issue is raised here or there? Isn't the problem really one of how to encourage students in the appropriation of a coherent *set* of values that can lead to satisfaction and a sense of purpose? And isn't it hard to imagine a coherent education for values amidst an incoherent curriculum?

As Rudolph (1962) shows in his fine history of the American college curriculum, the colonial and post-Revolutionary set curricula were based upon implicit (if changing) sets of values. After the Civil War, *electives* came into their own. This development was crucial for moving colleges into the mainstream of American life and for the development of the university, but the values of the elective system were individualism and progress. The notion that the curriculum should stress a common set of values was lost. Today, when students can fulfill the two-course humanities distribution requirement by taking symbolic logic and music appreciation or a year of Asian history, how can we speak of the invitation of the curriculum to engage in coherent and comprehensive thinking about values?

The shortcomings of distribution requirements for assuring an education for values is only one of the reasons that new courses on values are being introduced. Callahan and Bok—the directors of a recent Hastings Center project on the teaching of ethics—contend that beyond real or imagined shifts in student attitudes or liberal arts practice, *new issues* demand new initiatives. The issues, they write,

turn less on personal virtue than on the emergence of a number of exceedingly difficult ethical dilemmas, both within the society and within the professions. Tensions between freedom and justice, between individual autonomy and government regulation, between efficiency and equity, between privacy and a right to information, between the rights of individuals and the rights of society, have become more sharply focused. They have been expressed in a wide range of specific issues: abortion, termination of treatment of dying patients, whistle-blowing in the professions, conflict of interest among researchers and policymakers, questions of risks and benefits in assessing scientific, technological, and environmental issues, and the limits of paternalism in medicine, government, and the law. (Hastings Center, 1980:3)

Many of the new courses on ethics and values focus directly upon various dilemmas associated with these value conflicts.

Morrill (1982:66), another leading theoretician on the teaching of values, suggests the sorts of studies that are particularly rich for values education:

1. Social choices and cultural issues
2. Normative and professional ethics
3. Comparative cultural studies
4. Moral imagination in literary and artistic expression
5. Experiential and career education

There are broad opportunities for values education within a variety of curricular structures. The vocational preoccupations of students can be turned to the advantage of teaching values if serious examination of ethical dilemmas in the various professions is an entry point for reflection and the development of a broad sense of professional responsibility is the goal. As a friend of mine observed: "If I offer a course on 'Introduction to Ethics,' seven students will sign-up. If I offer 'Introduction to Medical Ethics for Pre-Meds,' I'll get thirty or forty."

HOW SHALL WE TEACH?

New developments in science, technology, and the professions, a new national concern for integrity in public life, and a resolve to combat individualistic narcissism all lead to a new interest in values education. Coinciding with this interest, new theoretical resources of two sorts are becoming available.

In the first place, new insights into *values development* in older adolescents and young adults is emerging from the work of William Perry, Lawrence Kohlberg, and Carol Gilligan in social and educational psychology (see Chickering, 1981). In general, the experimental work of these scholars indicates that students go through clearly recognizable stages in the development of their ability to make judgments and take courses of action that are fair, tolerant, and sensitive to the needs and rights of others. Presumably, a knowledge of the natural progression of values development can help a teacher work with, and not against, the student's emerging capabilities by setting challenges for growth that are rigorous but not impossible. Of course, to do so raises questions about knowing where students are located developmentally. The problem is complicated by the fact that the patterns of development may differ between the sexes, so that the right approach for women may be the wrong one for men. Needless to say, even students of the same sex in a given class may be at very different stages of moral development.

Specialists in moral development have attempted to address these problems, but real puzzles remain for the average faculty member. A deeper problem, however, is deciding how much responsibility one wants to take for trying to affect moral development directly. As opposed to the more limited vision of trying to raise values issues intellectually in ways that are accessible and engaging, do faculty members really want to take responsibility for behavior modification? This may be the case at some schools with a high degree of faculty/administrative consensus, a clear, values-laden ethos, and a tight curriculum—the widely publicized "valuing" competency requirement of Alverno College comes to mind. But at most schools, faculty desire to inculcate values (as opposed to raising issues) is limited to insisting that students buy into values like academic honesty and respect for competence.

Professionals in areas such as student affairs tend to be more conversant with the developmental literature than most faculty members, and hence these issues open promising areas for dialogue between persons having different roles in the college. At the same time I am skeptical as to whether the theoretical literature will have an enduring impact and consequences for classroom teaching unless the exploration of the implications is encouraged in faculty-driven professional development activities. Here again, naiveté won't fly. It's not very helpful to the literary scholar concerned with questions of the canon and preservation of our heritage to be told that late adolescents might "relate" more to *Romeo and Juliet* and older students more to *King Lear*. When faced with the serious question of deciding how to teach literature in ways that will disclose the far reaches of human passion, frailty, and dignity, suggestions at this level border upon the insulting.

The second theoretical source of values education which comes to bear upon current problems is the discipline of ethics, pursued as a field both within philosophy and the academic study of religion. The ongoing discussion of what principles *should* guide human conduct has been of inestimable significance in shaping the culture and values of the West. Indeed, one of the most common ways in which colleges traditionally have sought to shape values has been by confronting students with the theories of such thinkers as Aristotle, Kant, and Mill.

Ethics as a discipline involves a process of reasoning and the attempt to establish propositions about human conduct that might serve as guides to action. The emphasis in teaching formal ethics is not upon learning rules, but upon how to think carefully about moral problems. Articulating and defending reasons for decisions and actions is an important goal of the study of ethics. The goal is rarely perceived as behavior modification in any direct way. Rather, the hope is that students will become "more alert to perceiving ethical issues, more aware of the reasons underlying moral principles, and more equipped to reason carefully in applying these principles to concrete cases" (Hastings Center, 1980:7). The project on the teaching of ethics conducted by the Hastings Center Institute of Society, Ethics and Life Sciences, the work of Norman Bowie's Center for the Study of Values, the work on biomedical ethics of the Kennedy Institute at Georgetown University, and the endeavors of the Society for Values in Higher Education exemplify the approach rooted in philosophy and religious social ethics.

The Hastings Center report (1980:48–56) lists a series of goals for teaching ethics which is applicable to the teaching of values more generally. I find it helpful to think of these goals as a sequence of pedagogical steps and offer a few of my own comments under the headings proposed in the report:

1. *Stimulating the moral imagination.* Students must come to see "that human beings live in a web of moral relationships, that a consequence of moral positions and rules can be actual suffering or happiness, and that moral conflicts are frequently inevitable and difficult." The report speaks of helping students develop "the ability to gain a feeling for the lives of others" and of evoking "the emotional side of students.., [their] empathy, feeling, caring, sensibility." The report warns against simply *overloading* the imagination with novels, plays, films, and accounts of personal experience without also introducing a cognitive dimension. I am less concerned with the danger of runaway imagination. The need for moral imagination is acute, and I worry more about whether it holds the place it deserves among the critical thinking skills we seek to develop in students. Further, internships, field-based experiences, and work-study programs in which students confront other languages, cultures, and economic conditions supplement imagination as a stimulus for moral reflection.

2. *Recognizing ethical issues.* The stimulation of feeling should lead to an attempt to sort out moral issues. At this point, skills in cognition and expression come directly into play.

3. *Developing analytic skills.* The report notes that reflection on moral issues requires the development of skills in using concepts such as *justice, autonomy, dignity,* and *rights*. I believe that similar skills in working with concepts are needed in other value areas, such as the ability to deal with aesthetic values in terms of *beauty, experience,* and *art*. Concepts of *intent* and *consequence* are necessary in both the moral and the aesthetic realms of values.

4. *Eliciting a sense of moral obligation and personal responsibility.* The report asserts that any course on ethics must raise the question of "Why ought I to be moral?" This leads to discussion of the reality of human freedom, of having options and responsibility.

5. *Tolerating—and resisting—disagreement and ambiguity.* The key is to help students accept the ambiguity and complexity of values dilemmas without falling into sheer relativism. Values are ultimately patterns of personal choice, but this is not to say that all choices are equally defensible, or that the value choices of others— in history, in our culture, and in other cultures—cannot help us

in making our own choices in pursuing a life of purpose and meaning. At this stage the articulation of issues, the analysis of options, and a coherent defense of the ultimately personal and existential choices we must make is intellectually demanding to the highest degree.

Values are conservative. As the patterns of choice by which we act, they help us persevere in a course of conduct despite the uncertainties and ambiguities which characterize existence. The ability to *articulate* our values serves to remind us of the choices we have actually made and the investment of our selves as family members, professionals, and citizens. Careful, coherent, imaginative reflection on values dispels the notion that our choices are whimsical or can be shifted without consequence.

Richard Morrill's (1982) outline of the pedagogy of teaching values stresses the development of the same three skills of imagination, analysis, and expression. For Morrill (1982:52–60), the steps are:

1. *Value analysis.* In a situation of choice, what seem to be the stakes in terms of human well-being? What appeals to ultimate principles of individual and social good undergird conflicting positions? Morrill observes that values

   analysis is not an isolated technique, cut off from an interest in beliefs, myths, principles, laws, institutions, and factual circumstances.... (Values analysis) might lead to an extended consideration of the underlying vision of human nature and destiny, or require that there be a fuller exploration of factual conditions. The conclusions that are reached in values analysis require, of course, various types of evidence and warrants, much as in any form of critical inquiry. These conclusions are descriptive statements about what values are present in a situation. They are not specific value judgments that such and such is the case or should be done. Values analysis could indeed prepare the way and provide the backing for value judgments, but the latter require a different and distinctive step.

2. *Values consciousness.* Here Morrill refers to a "moment" of vivifying which enhances the imaginative grasp of the meaning of values. "Finding values, I find the person, for they regulate the

personal center from which choice and action flow." Is this not how we experience our own values, as standards which guide our choices? For Morrill, this center of the self is conscience, not understood as "the guilt-ridden part of the self" but as "the self's process of critical self-appraisal and self-judgment"—a form of self-consciousness—and the object of values education.

3. *Values criticism.* At this level of inquiry, analysis of conflicts and competing claims is enriched by the vivid sense of the centrality of values in our identity, in order to pose normative questions about options and choices (without necessarily coming to specific answers). Morrill holds that this critical task is particularly appropriate to the college. "The pedagogical aim of values criticism is to develop in students an internalized capacity for the self-criticism of values—that is, to educate conscience."

Morrill (1982:61–62) further proposes general criteria for valuing. Here, the student examines whether his or her judgments are:

1. Consistent and capable of universal application
2. Coherent with the totality of his or her life
3. Comprehensive and sustainable over time
4. Adequate (by contributing to satisfaction and fulfillment)
5. Authentic and open

Morrill (1982:65) contends the pedagogical implications of his approach are "significant but not radical." Many college instructors regularly use approaches to issues roughly parallel to his steps of analysis, consciousness, and criticism. The important thing is that values education cannot be passive. Students must be stimulated to take an active role in framing and articulating their views. They must be encouraged to persevere in seeking insights about difficult problems and be "challenged to dig deeply for the final justifications for human choices" (Morrill, 1982:65).

One can imagine the sort of lively, tough dialogue that Morrill and the Hastings Center scholars envision. Whether we can create this in our own classrooms depends, in part, upon our general skills in establishing and leading discussions (see

Kasulis, 1982). Beyond these general skills, values pedagogy requires that the teacher risk revealing and discussing his or her own values and take the lead in the critical analysis of deeply held convictions.

Some specific strategies deserve mention. The power of fiction and film to stimulate the moral imagination has been previously noted. Often structured case studies and simulations can prompt the open, critical and subtle discussion of value issues and conflicts. Among the many elements that contribute to exciting values-oriented discussions are:

1. Careful choice of materials
2. Thorough mastery of the readings and relevant data
3. Preparation of alternative scenarios for class discussion; anticipating the variety of worthwhile directions a discussion might go; being flexible without getting off the track
4. Constant awareness of the participants as the basis for encouraging (or limiting) the contributions from specific individuals
5. Timing—including the ability to restate, summarize, and use humor in a limited and controlled fashion at appropriate points.

SUMMARY

New dilemmas posed by advances in technology and new demands for accountability in personal and professional life have established a need for critical and imaginative thinking about values that is both rigorous and extensive. Values education that will meet these needs involves strengthening the moral imagination of students, nurturing their ability to analyze values issues carefully, and providing them with opportunities to articulate well-considered positions with courage and tolerance.

Small colleges have the resources and usually the institutional commitment to conduct effective values education, but broad and challenging questions require ongoing dialogue: *Which* values shall we focus upon for special examination and nurture? *Where* in the curriculum shall we concentrate attention upon values? *How* shall we educate? If the college experience is to include an "education of conscience," faculty members and administrators must work together to support an institutional ethos of community, a coherent curriculum, and a pedagogy which creates active engagement between teacher and students in exploring the deepest questions of human motivation and purpose.

6

Implementing a Small College Computer Planning Committee: Recommendations and Caveats

ROBERT L. WARD

Historically, academic computing has meant programming. Computing has been perceived as affecting only those students and faculty in departments where programming was taught—usually computer science, math, engineering, and business. Thus the interests and needs of these departments decided the shape of the campus computing facilities, usually through a single parent department's normal decision making process.

Now the widespread acceptance of office automation technologies and the anticipated application of artificial intelligence techniques to routine decision making have created a campus-wide need for computing resources. Academic computing is now a concern of the entire student and faculty population (Bradley and Williams, 1982). Providing adequate computing resources on such a wide scale can easily consume hundreds of thousands and even millions of dollars (Adams, 1984; Bray, 1984). The implication in an era of constrained budgets is that other facilities will suffer. Clearly, ad hoc, single department planning and decision making are no longer appropriate.

This paper addresses the process of long-range, campus-wide planning for academic computing in the small college environment, where computing expertise may be scarce and some faculty may be resistant to change. The target campus has limited experience with computing (perhaps a fledgling computer science department with one or two faculty members) and is feeling considerable pressure to "computerize" (perhaps from alumni, incoming students, or innovative faculty). The material here does not identify the "best" computers, software, and peripherals, but rather attempts to equip the reader to develop a computing facility well-suited to the needs of such a campus by sketching an appropriate procedural framework, identifying some of the major issues, warning about the most dangerous pitfalls, and offering some generally applicable advice.

On-campus computer expertise in the form of a computer science department, data processing major, or administrative computing facility provides critical support to the planning process. Readers employed at colleges that lack any on-campus computing expertise may want to consult Hughes (1983) or the suggestions for faculty development which appear later in this chapter. (Although aimed at high school environments, Hughes's suggestions are still appropriate.)

THE PLANNING BODY

The first step is to establish a new planning committee. Computer planning tasks are too large, diverse, and encumbered with territorial encroachments to be handled effectively by any existing body. Committee members should possess:

1. Viewpoints representative of the campus-at-large
2. Management expertise
3. Computing expertise
4. Peer group credibility
5. A commitment to the task (see Brady, 1984)

The group should be representative and credible to ensure that the result is acceptable to the campus-at-large. Management expertise will be necessary if computing-induced changes in communication patterns and in the distribution of authority and control are to be anticipated and effectively managed (Attewel and Rule, 1984). Technical expertise will tend to confine the discussion to that which is feasible. A useful plan will demand some serious research (mostly outside individual committee member's specialties) and some territorial largess by all the committee members, making a high level of commitment essential.

Small committees, of course, work most effectively. Unfortunately, the task is probably too large for two or three persons to tackle alone. A two-level structure (committee and executive committee or committee and support personnel) offers a good compromise, preserving the focus and coherence of a small committee, but ensuring the representative perspective and larger work force of a larger committee.

Even with the support of a large committee, it will probably be necessary to schedule release time for the committee chairperson and at least one technical member. Naming a highly committed, nontechnical member as chairperson effectively underscores the difference between campus planning and computer science departmental planning (and may increase campuswide acceptance of the committee).

The coherence and vision of the resulting plan will depend, in short, on whether the body develops a group personality and a sense of mission. Attendance, en masse, at an appropriate conference often fosters this esprit de corps. Alternatively (or additionally), the committee could visit campuses with more developed academic computing programs (Hughes, 1983).

The planning body will require formal communication channels with diverse campus structures. It should raise policy issues directly with the faculty-at-large. Projected budgets should be disseminated via the administration. Direct student, faculty, and departmental surveys may be appropriate. Occasional interviews with administrative staff will assist in formulating plans for new support structures. Final recommendations should reach the faculty and administration through existing campuswide long-range planning structures.

THE PLANNING PROCESS

The Charge

The planning body must have a clear statement of its mission, either from without or of its own construction. To create a base for its subsequent work, the committee should begin by inventorying present resources and needs, projecting future needs, and identifying emerging policy issues (see Komoski, 1983, for some guidelines). Next, the committee should write a handful of long-term goals, striving to address the most important needs identified during the first phase and keeping the institutional mission firmly in mind. Finally the committee should draft specific objectives which will contribute to meeting the agreed-upon goals. Viewed collectively, the objectives will become the plan of action for the college (Brady, 1984).

Good planning strives for a careful balance between creativity and realism (Shank, Niblock, and Sandalls, Jr., 1975). The order set out above is significant because it encourages the development of creative goals before heightening the planners' awareness of real-world limitations. Similarly it is important that the planning body not be charged with day-to-day operational management of an existing or developing computing facility. Routine involvement with day-to-day operations tends to replace goal-oriented planning with more urgent problem-response behavior.

Although continuous in nature (Brady, 1984), long-range planning should be undertaken as though the process were close-ended—the committee should produce a document or series of documents by a fixed date. The importance of a well-written document cannot be underestimated. Indeed, the committee would be wise to consider hiring a consultant specifically to draft the document after completing the balance of its work (Holtz, 1983). Without a written document, the committee's only product is nebulous debate. With a written document, the committee equips administrators to carry the plan to the college's constituents, write job descriptions, seek equipment bids, apply for grants, and adjust related long-range plans.

The Inventory

The inventory should attempt far more than a listing of equipment and software, though that is important. Ideally the inventory should enlighten the planner as a literature survey enlightens the beginning researcher. The objective is to uncover and understand key relationships among the components of the campus and the computing facility.

Study the Nature of User Demand and Expectation. Computer usage patters add another layer of complexity to the campus social structure. An analysis which focuses only on institutional roles (students vis-a-vis faculty and staff) will obscure many important differences among users and overlook important trends in usage. For a better understanding, the planners should focus on differences in applications, in user work habits, and in user computing experience.

Because each application makes different demands for system resources, planners need to know how users distribute their time among typical applications. In the domain of office automation these include word processing, spread sheets, database manipulation, and electronic mail. In the instructional domain are courseware authoring, program development (for computer science students), computer-assisted instruction (CAI here meaning drill and practice), training simulations, practice with real-world systems (computer-aided design—CAD—stations, accounting packages), and instructor support systems (e.g., grading and record-keeping). In the research domain are the use of statistical packages, simulation languages for modeling, data base manipulation, data acquisition, and special-purpose analytic packages. Planners should be aware that applications bearing the same label are not always functionally equivalent. Students in an introductory statistics class, for example, may be well served by a statistics package of limited numerical accuracy. Faculty researchers may demand a package of much greater accuracy. Thus, the most useful application morphologies are based on functionality.

User preferences vary widely, and planners should expect users to mold the computing facility, not vice versa (Hiltz, 1982). It is important to know when, where, with whom, and for how long users prefer to work and to understand how these preferences are related to user experience and specific applications. Preference will vary by time of day as well as by day of the week. Some will confine themselves to a single application per session, others will change rapidly from application to application within the same session. Users are also social animals and will exhibit varying preferences for working alone or in select groups.

These factors are seldom independent, and relationships often influence the total design of the facilities. Novices, for example, tend to be more comfortable working in groups where help abounds. Proficient users prefer to move the work into a more conventional environment—faculty and staff to their offices, students to dormitories or the library. The obvious implication is that beginning users should be serviced in large labs staffed with "consultants." The relationship between experienced and novice users within an application can also be an important indicator of future needs within that application.

In time-shared systems, much of this information can be captured by the operating system accounting package. Properly designed sign-up sheets can capture the same information in microcomputer labs. These collection mechanisms have the advantage of being unobtrusive, inexpensive, and reliable. Unfortunately they select only current users. Surveys are probably the only way to build an estimate of how nonusers will eventually affect demand (if at all). While difficult to manage, surveys are nevertheless unobtrusive and inexpensive. (For example, students could complete a questionnaire as part of course enrollment or the normal advising process.)

Detail Locus of Responsibility. This item and the one that follows will tell whether or not computing support structures are sufficiently organized to allow good management control. Computing activities imply at least the following responsibilities: selection of standards for equipment and program interface; equipment and software evaluation; equipment and software specification, purchasing, and receiving; software license negotiation; equipment and software installation; faculty and student training (both for instructional and noninstructional uses); software, software license, and documentation archiving and cataloging; identifying equipment and software failures; equipment maintenance; software maintenance; documentation maintenance; documentation distribution; housekeeping (including cleaning terminals, replacing ribbons, and collecting discarded paper); courseware development; use regulation (sign-up sheets, security, food-and-drink monitoring, and so on); user assistance; and equipment supervision and operation (in time-shared operations).

In many cases responsibility for these various tasks will be divided among several persons. If so, the division will as likely be by application, experience, or work habits as by institutional role.

Identify Existing Computing Policies. A set of operational policies usually accompanies each of the above responsibilities. Other more general policies are important, too: access for handi-capped students, discipline for equipment theft or vandalism, position on software piracy, access for poor students (in environments with lab fees), access preferences based on institutional roles, discipline for cheating by copying another student's files, and discipline for other more subtle exploitations of security deficiencies.

Produce a List of Resources. A useful list should survey such resources as: plant facilities, teaching materials, equipment by function, software by application and target machine, software expertise by specialty or vendor, documentation, vendor literature, and possible consultants by specialty. Functional classifications will be particularly important in performing the following analysis.

Assess the Match Between Function and Functionality. The objective here is to evaluate the appropriateness of given resources to the function they are performing. Excess functionality results in direct waste of resources, yet, functionality that is too restricted results in inefficiency and indirect waste of resources.

Word processing, for example, significantly underutilizes the capabilities of an IBM PC with 500KB of main memory, a 10MB hard disk, a math co-processor, and high resolution color graphics. On the other hand time-shared program development generally taxes the functionality of an 8-bit microcomputer.

Similar mismatches can be present in software use. For example, in a typical limited memory, time-shared mini computer environment it would usually be inappropriate to give beginning programming students access only to an editor that is configured as a single (memory intensive) load-module if the same editor were available configured as several overlays (less memory intensive). The opposite would probably be true in a disk-limited microcomputer environment.

Appropriateness tests can and should be applied to administrative structures, policies, and training programs as well.

The Target

Next the committee must quantify its vision of the future, a process that defies step-by-step description. The final result, however, must be a quantified description of the anticipated role of academic computing at the end of the planning interval—a portrait of the target toward which the plan will aim. It should be realistic, allowing for ungovernable demands identified during the inventory and yet idealistic, expecting to manage controllable demands (Shank, Niblock, and Sandalls, Jr., 1975). It must describe a future consistent with the tradition of the institution (Masland, 1984), but one reached along a path of enlightened evolution.

The starting point should be an estimate of future demands. The eventual result will be a detailed list of objectives, which describes equipment, software, staff and faculty responsibilities, and important characteristics of the projected campus population.

Forecasting Demand. Simply stated, there is no rule for projecting demand—computing demand is too strongly influenced by unpredictable external forces and too complex to be modeled accurately (Moyer, 1984), even if the institution has adequate baseline data, which it probably does not. The planning committee, relying on its collective intuition, sense of campus history, and the data collected during the inventory, must make an educated guess at the important parameters for each significant application. Surprisingly, if the committee members have sufficient expertise about their campus, their intuition

stands an excellent chance of being reasonably accurate
(Chambers, Mullick, and Smith, 1971).

The structure of the final forecast should mirror the structure
of the inventory. Eventual demand should be stated in terms
of resources required by each segment of the user community,
identified by application, work habits, and experience. Underlying assumptions about usage trends should be clearly ex-
plained as an aid to later performance monitoring. Finally,
aggregate demand, measured in terminal hours per student
per week, file space per user, or some other appropriate metric,
should be compared to usage levels reported by other colleges.
Bray (1984), for example, reports that at Clarkson College students average five terminal hours per week.

Drafting Goals. Goals—by which planners mean long-term outcomes—should be only as specific as necessary to guide the
later drafting of objectives. For a small liberal arts college,
goals should address such questions as: What is the relationship between liberal arts and academic computing? What computing resources should the college provide to faculty, students,
and staff? Goals should broadly state what is to be accomplished; objectives will outline the shape of the implementation. The temptation will be to determine not only goals, but
also the means by which they are reached. A total separation
of result from method is clearly impossible, but methods are
more readily engineered than goals and thus should be fixed
as late in the process as reasonable.

Goals can be surprisingly difficult to distinguish from objectives, especially when they involve personnel. Examining the
life of a proposed goal may clarify its nature. Goals usually
describe long-lived responsibilities and facilities—support for
needs which outlive the planning interval. For example, making comprehensive documentation readily available to all users
is clearly a proper goal—it describes an effect which presumably outlives the life of the plan. The initial development of
specific manuals, however, is a transient task and is best detailed when objectives are drafted. If instead a staff position
(technical writer) were included as a goal, several reasonable
implementation alternatives (e.g., hiring a consulting techni-

cal writer or purchasing commercial versions) would be excluded prematurely.

Some authors have argued that the distinction between goals and objectives is arbitrary (Mace, 1975). But in the diverse environment of the small college, it is useful to set goals first, so that fundamental differences over priorities may be debated before the complexities of ease of implementation are addressed. To keep this debate manageable, planners should deliberately restrict themselves to a small number of goals.

Drafting Objectives. Once goals have been drafted, the planners should turn to the task of constructing supporting objectives. Objectives (coupled with action plans) are what most persons associate with planning. Objectives must include a timetable for the acquisition of equipment, software, and new staff and faculty, and for the training or retraining of existing staff and faculty. They should indicate where responsibility for key functions will reside and explain how each contributes to the proper functioning of the anticipated infrastructure. Objectives (unlike the earlier goal-setting phase) should strive to be immensely realistic, tempering goals to meet budgetary constraints, scheduling easily managed and urgent tasks early, and delaying the difficult and superfluous ones. The objectives alone should detail temporary structures and explain how they contribute to the development of appropriate support structures or the acquisition of needed resources.

Well-written objectives are cohesive, functional, and clearly related to user demand and to previously established planning goals. As an example:

Objective Ten—Unrestricted access Word processing: supported via a cluster of six floppy disk–based word-processing stations available on short notice sign-up and monitored 24 hours a day. Each stand-alone station will provide a full typewriter keyboard, a business text CRT, dual disk drives, in RAM editing of at least a 30-page (30k) document, access to a shared draft printer, access to the campus network, and access to a shared formed character printer. Supporting software will be disk-resident and checked out through the monitor. Applications receiving institutional support will be word processing, spread sheets, simple relational data bases, and terminal emulation. The monitor will be thoroughly trained in the use of all institutionally supported software and charged with assisting users on request. Each station should be able to read at least one of the three institutionally supported disk formats.

Provided that terms like "full typewriter keyboard" and "draft printer" are defined carefully elsewhere in the document, this example illustrates several important characteristics of a well-written objective. It is totally functional. It addresses a cohesive set of applications (office automation). Its relationship to user work habits and expertise is clear (public, open 24 hours, support for novices, group situation). The amount of demand serviced is quantified (six units, two shared printers). In short the appropriateness of the objective to the estimated demands and planning goals should be easy to gauge.

Important functional relationships between this objective and other objectives are also specified. Compatibility with other equipment is addressed explicitly (disk formats, network interface), and presumably other compatibility issues (e.g., word-processor file structures) would be addressed indirectly through the definitions mentioned above. An accompanying overview should clarify the significance of these relationships in the planners' vision.

Note that no date has been set for achieving this objective. The first draft of the objectives should indicate only dependency relationships (which objectives are prerequisites to accomplishing others). Eventually a timetable for all objectives must be detailed, but delaying the timetable until all objectives are established allows each to be considered in context. Indeed, limited resources will normally force low-priority or low-demand objectives to be tabled.

Many objectives will describe job functions. An objective describing the monitor's responsibilities should accompany the above objective. Other objectives should describe purchasing, maintenance, and supervisory functions implied by equipment-oriented objectives. Unrelated tasks and responsibilities should not be combined in the same objective description. Later, as the plan is implemented, related objectives will be collected into reasonable packages and turned into job descriptions.

Implementation and Evaluation. Eventually persons must be chosen to draw action plans to guide the implementation of the objectives and monitor performance. Some authors (e. g., Brady, 1984) make both tasks the responsibilities of the planning body. In contrast, I consider action planning to be the proper domain of the administration (or perhaps of an operations committee or manager). If the planning committee is to exist even after a plan is drafted, then it should monitor the implementation performance and accuracy of its forecasts and modify objectives when necessary. The continuing function of the committee, however, is beyond the scope of this paper.

GUIDING PRINCIPLES

The principles mentioned below assume something of an engineering bias. Specifically, they assume that the objective of long-range planning is to achieve maximum effect at minimum cost. Cost and effect are defined broadly, however, in an effort to address the role of second-order effects.

Expect Change

Any practical long-term plan must allow for panoramic change. Hardware will continue to benefit from improved circuit technology, though perhaps at a slightly lessened pace (Lerner, 1984). Increasing architectural sophistication will support improved performance with any specific level of technology. Mass storage devices will continue to evolve, exhibiting ever-increasing density and speed (Killmon, 1984). Peripherals will continue to acquire more and more intelligence and functionality. Distributed processing and multiprocessors may significantly improve the price/performance ratio during the next three to five years (for example, see Awalt and Gee, 1983).

Software will also change. For one thing, availability will continue to improve, though distribution format may change significantly. New copy-protection schemes, availability of low-cost software in certain markets, and increased use of public packet-switched networks will all affect trends in distribution systems.

Fundamental advances in software technology will also stimulate change. Artificial intelligence techniques (sometimes made practical by hardware improvements) will stimulate improvements in the user interface and support ever more sophisticated interactions between user and software (Manuel and Evanczuk, 1983). Program generators, expert systems, and natural language interfaces will soon follow word processors (*Business Week*, 1984).

Users will change, exhibiting increased sophistication and steadily increasing expectations. Future users will not only be trained in specific applications earlier (e.g., word processing), but will have a greater awareness of the general applicability of computing. Each successful application of computing will contribute to rising user expectations for future applications. Increased exposure to software will heighten an appreciation for quality in software, generating changes in the software market. In particular, we should see significantly more effective models for the user interface (e.g., Macintosh).

Development and refinement of standards will continue to act as a stimulus for change. Some of these changes will be evolutionary and thus somewhat predictable. Others, usually de facto standards imposed by major manufacturers (e.g., IBM's strangely located shift key and selection of MS/DOS) will seem arbitrary to all except industry insiders. Broader use will undoubtedly bring additional federal regulation, at least for the near future.

Application program standards, now only a developing trend, will probably become a major market force (Hindin, 1983). Presently evident mostly as vendor-imposed standards (e.g., Wordstar files), soon there should be widely accepted standards for terminal interfaces (McGregor and Lewis, 1983), file formats (for diverse applications), and for operating system program services (analogous to existing standards for network program services, see Irvine and Overgaard, 1983).

Plan for Flexibility

Avoid Vendor Dependence. This often-given advice is frequently misunderstood as an admonishment to avoid vendors who may go bankrupt. Indeed, one should give preference to reliable vendors, but in a market as volatile as computing such vendors are often hard to spot. (Even IBM has found itself forced out of certain markets from time to time.) Any time a vendor's decision to change its product or product support significantly impairs your ability to implement a plan, then the plan is vendor-dependent.

Some forms of vendor dependence are quite insidious, in part because they constitute historically acceptable management practice. For example, it is common for large commercial computing installations to develop all their software to run under their prime vendor's operating system. Unfortunately, if the vendor fails, decides to support a different operating system, or perhaps just changes one or two features in the existing system, all dependent software must be abandoned or rewritten. A similar pitfall awaits anyone developing systems dependent on vendor-specific features in terminals, printers, plotters, disk drives, or any other products.

Some vendors (IBM for example) have a reputation for never throwing out anything that might affect their user's software, a practice advertised as mitigating the deleterious effects of vender dependence. Unfortunately, even stability in the vendor's products and services doesn't eliminate the potential for disastrous consequences. Users often wish to move software to another vendor's hardware for reasons not related to the vendor's performance. Perhaps they wish to move an application from the mainframe to a microcomputer, or perhaps from an expensive leased system to some recently donated hardware. The bottom line is that vendor dependence nearly always reduces flexibility and consequently should nearly always be avoided.

One avoids vendor dependence, in part, by acquiring control of the virtual environment. Application programs expect the operating system and hardware to do certain tasks for them. This set of tasks constitutes the virtual environment. One controls this environment by specifying a commonly available set of capabilities and purchasing (or writing) only that software which uses only the defined capabilities (Hall, Sherrer, and Sventek, 1980). To a limited extent, this is the effect of committing to UNIX, MS/DOS, CP/M, or some other operating system supported by many vendors (Dalrymple, 1984).

Build a System That Fails Gracefully. Computing systems, even microcomputers, fail. As computing resources become integral with the campus, it becomes crucial that such failures have restricted impact. Key components should have standby backup or the ability to operate in a reduced configuration. A time-shared mainframe, for example, might be backed up by a high-speed communication line to a similar installation (provided similar software was available there). An eight-card multiplexer might still operate with only six functioning cards.

Here decentralized systems have a distinct advantage. A lab equipped with several stand-alone microcomputers, for example, still services students well despite the failure of a single processor. (Microcomputers are not *ipso facto* decentralized. Commonly, teaching labs operate several microcomputers from a single disk or print sharer. Clearly the failure of the disk server leaves the microcomputer stations useless, or at least much less usable.)

Opt for Mixed Mode Solutions. There is no single optimal response to computing needs. A group of disk-less microcomputers sharing a single disk server is more economical than a group of stand-alone disk-based machines, but the stand-alone machines offer greater fault tolerance. Each decision involves a trade-off; the best compromise usually involves a little of each extreme (for example, a lab with disk-less and disk-based microcomputers all attached to a disk server).

Set Minimum Standards to Ensure Cross-Functionality. Computers usually outlive their intended application. Requiring each to meet some least common denominator of functionality improves the practicality of successfully applying machines to unanticipated tasks (especially if the defined virtual environment and minimum standards are identical or nearly so). Of particular importance are equipment interface standards. Requiring that all machines conform to one or two interface standards (e.g., RS 232 serial or Centronics parallel) facilitates reconfiguration. Similarly, requiring all machines to provide at least an 80 by 24 display and a full typewriter keyboard encourages diverse use of equipment and development and acquisition of portable software.

Pay Close Attention to the Computing Infrastructure

The delivery mechanism determines how accessible resources are to users and thus is crucial to user satisfaction. Accessibility is determined by more than just equipment availability. Application file compatibility, the accuracy and availability of documentation, timely response to failures (hardware and software), housekeeping, public awareness of resources, physical location and work environment, the consistency of the user interface from one application to another, the availability of personal assistance, electronic communications, guidance in software selection, assistance in software installation, and timely availability of training all affect the usability of computing resources.

Documentation, user assistance, public awareness, and equipment maintenance deserve particular attention. Responsibility for acquiring, maintaining, and distributing documentation; for recruiting, training, and supervising user assistance; for maintaining public awareness of computing resources; and for reporting, logging, and servicing failed hardware and software must be clearly outlined.

A carefully designed infrastructure can significantly reduce the cost of computing resources. Keen and Woodman (1984) estimate the real cost of a personal computer-based business work station is $26,000—average cost for direct hardware and software is $7,000, indirect computing and communications cost is $11,000, and support cost is $8,000. Clearly, reducing the cost of support and communications can have a significant impact on the real cost of the resources.

Be Aware of Second-Order Effects

Planners must be alert to potential second-order effects. The college campus is a complex, highly coupled system, and academic computing implies large-scale change; the full ramifications of such change are not obvious. For example, part-time secretarial work is an important ingredient in many student financial aid packages. If the availability of word processing to faculty reduces the demand for student secretaries, financial aid and student recruitment could suffer. At first glance, academic computing appears to offer many opportunities for replacement student jobs, but these new positions may not entail the same student–professor relationship—conceivably student (or even faculty) retention could suffer.

Develop Appropriate Management Expertise

Management of computing resources is replete with its own unique problems. More decision making relies on low-level personnel (Pfeffer, 1981), equipment has a short life, and effective equipment use sometimes depends on the equivalent of research and development. For many persons computing is threatening. Computing changes job content, affects job security (Attewell and Rule, 1984), and is widely associated with frighteningly esoteric math and engineering skills. These problems must be addressed through careful, sensitive, and timely management. Appropriate training for key administrators and planners should lead the training agenda. Dight (1984) lists several firms specializing in related training and gives guidelines for selecting training programs.

Don't Overlook the Cost of Software

It is literally true that the cost of software over the life of a computer can run several times more than the machine. Personal computers (Zorba, Compaq, IBM PC Junior, Apple IIc) are routinely available for $700 to $1,000. Commercial software costs almost as much per package (for example, dBASE III, LOTUS Symphony, and Dow Jones Market Microscope cost between $475 and $499). In most cases substantial educational discounts (often 80 percent) and special institutional licenses (buy one and use it everywhere) are available, but even so, acquiring a large repertoire of software for each work station on campus is expensive.

In part because of software costs, the price/performance battle between single-user microcomputers and time-shared minicomputers and super-microcomputers is not quite as decided as many believe. For example, a twelve-station 68000 based multi-user system equipped with five different languages can be purchased for about $3,700 per station, which compares quite favorably with fully equipped IBM PCs.

Don't Overlook the Importance of Communications

Planners must recognize that communications is crucial to the most widely sought computing application—office automation. Keen and Woodman (1984) maintain that the "key development in the micro field is not . . . in hardware or applications software but in the addition of a communications capability." McFarlan, McKenney, and Pyburn (1983) observe that computing, communications, and office automation are frequently managed as a block because of their strong similarities.

Typically, institutions initially acquire computing capacity, and particularly personal computers, to function as stand-alone solutions to specific problems. Eventually increased experience and user sophistication will foster interconnection between these stand-alone solutions (McFarlan, McKenney, and Pyburn, 1983). Gibson and Nolan (1974) refer to this transition from isolated solutions to integrated systems as formalization. Generally formalization is an expensive and painful experience for the institution. Plans that include adequate standards for communications can reduce both the cost and institutional trauma associated with this phase.

Planners should anticipate formalization by defining a long-term technical architecture for the entire computing plant, including microcomputers as one component (Keen and Woodman, 1984). This architecture should indicate the planners' preference for a local area network standard, for terminal communications standards, and for disk formats and file standards. Unfortunately data communications is a highly technical topic; local area network standards are just beginning to emerge; and disk and file standards are all but nonexistent. Access to a competent consultant or an attached engineering department becomes mandatory.

Design a Serious Faculty Development Program

A plan's success depends heavily upon faculty acceptance and participation. Successful faculty training programs reported in the literature have several common features. First, faculty usually train faculty, either in team projects (Mikkelson and Green, 1983) or traditional classroom settings (Harrow, 1982). Second, on campuses with limited technical expertise, external consultants are involved, in part to ensure that a professional quality program is developed. Consultants can assist in the planning (Buckner and Haugen, 1983), teach a "seed" team, orient administrative personnel, or assist faculty in designing course materials. Third, ample user support is provided either through student research assistants or through small groups working in lab environments (Buchner and Haugen, 1983; Mikkelson and Green, 1983; Killian, 1985). Fourth, significant amounts of release time are granted faculty charged with designing the development courses.

Buy Mature Technology

The newest, fastest, shiniest equipment seldom offers the best price/performance trade-off. New technology tends to be less reliable and more expensive (Riggs, 1983); the supporting software market is always underdeveloped. New products, however, don't always sport new technology. A new model computer, built with the same microprocessor used in hundreds of other models, is not usually new technology. Conversely, old products don't necessarily represent mature (as opposed to obsolete) technology. In most cases, if the technology has been available for two or three years and the product is in its third or fourth design iteration (model refinement), then it qualifies as mature technology.

Consider Free Software

If there is one exception to the adage "you get what you pay for," it is public domain software. Indeed there are worthless programs in the public domain, but there is also an amazing amount of professional quality software in the hands of users' groups and universities. Most hardware and software vendors include information about related users' groups in their documentation. Maintaining contact with all such users' groups is an important part of fully utilizing the product. (Several major users' groups are listed in this chapter's appendix.)

Software developed in graduate programs is available for a nominal fee from most major universities. To acquire the software, however, one must contact the custodian (often the author or advisor). Contacting the director of academic computing is sometimes productive (when a comprehesive index exists). Alternatively, specific teaching programs are regularly described by the authors in *ACM SIGSCE* and similar publications (e.g., Dodrill, 1982; Kerridge, 1982).

CONCLUSION

Perhaps more so than in other areas, long-range planning for computing is largely an exercise in educated guessing. One can never anticipate all the side effects or project exactly the full range of needs. Perhaps this realization more than anything else demands that liberal arts faculty be fully involved. Who could be better prepared to make "fuzzy" decisions based on limited information concerning an institution's present and future needs?

APPENDIX: SOME RESOURCES

The following organizations are interested in computer literacy and the campus-wide application of academic computing (from Levin, 1983).

Association for Computing Machinery (ACM)
1133 Avenue of the Americas
New York, New York
10036

Human Resources Research Organization
300 North Washington Street
Alexandria, Virginia
22314

International Council for Computers In Education
Department of Computer and Information Science
University of Oregon
Eugene, Oregon
97493

Microcomputer Resource Center
Teachers College
Columbia University
525 West 121st Street
New York, New York
10027

Microsoft
Northwest Regional Educational Laboratory
300 Southwest 6th Avenue
Portland, Oregon
97204

Minnesota Educational Computing Consortium
3250 Broadway Drive
St. Paul, Minnesota
55133

National Council of Teachers of Mathematics
1906 Association Drive
Reston, Virginia
22091

National Science Teachers Association
1742 Connecticut Avenue, N.W.
Washington, D.C.
20009

Users' groups can be an important source of software and
applications information for more knowledgeable microcom-

puter users. The following users' groups have important libraries of public domain software (for a more comprehensive list, see Froehlich, 1984).

CP/M Users' Group
1651 Third Avenue
New York, New York
10028

The C Users' Group
415 East Euclid Street
McPherson, Kansas
67460

Digital Equipment Computer Users Society
One Iron Way
Marlboro, Massachusetts
01752

Pascal Users' Group
Box 888524
Atlanta, Georgia
30338

SIG/M
Box 2085
177 Hadley Avenue
Clifton, New Jersey
07015–2085

Software Tools Users' Group
140 Center Street
El Segundo, California
90245

The computing market is changing so rapidly and is so diverse that merely identifying potential vendors is often an overwhelming task. *ComputerWorld* publishes annual buyers' guides which can be very helpful. (Recent guides have reviewed microcomputers and large system software.) *Mini-Micro Systems* frequently publishes product summaries in wide-ranging areas (see Hirsch, 1983; Kenealy, 1983; Stieffel and Simpson, 1983; Simpson, 1984). Brief reviews of individual products are available in *The Whole Earth Software Catalog* (Brand, 1984). Extensive product reviews and evaluations are available in a wide-ranging series of management reports from DataPro Research Corporation (1805 Underwood Boulevard, Delran, New Jersey 08075). These reports are relatively expensive (from $400 to $900), but are comprehensive and very usable.

7

Teaching Outside One's Areas of Expertise: Some Tips for Concealing "The Professor Has No Clothes"

RICHARD A. WRIGHT

When the uninformed Professor walked into the classroom and began lecturing, the upperclassmen exclaimed: "How intelligent the Professor's lectures are! And they are relevant to perfection!"

No upperclassman would disclose the lecture was inane, for fear of losing an "A."

None of the Professor's previous lectures had been so well-received!

"But he's got nothing to say," shouted a freshman in the last row. And eventually laughter and nodding agreement filled the classroom.

The Professor writhed, for he knew it was true. But he thought, "The lecture must go on." So he held himself stiffer at the podium, read the remainder of his lecture notes verbatim, and then beat a hasty retreat to his office to write a particularly difficult and vengeful midterm exam. (Adapted from "The Emperor's New Clothes"—with apologies to Hans Christian Andersen)

As a sociology graduate student at a large midwestern university, it was my mixed blessing to serve on a committee screening applicants for new faculty positions. Several criteria were used to expedite the rejection of unqualified applicants, including the nearly sacrosanct "four areas of specialization rule." The committee chair argued that it was impossible to achieve proficiency in more than four areas in sociology, so, for example, applicants listing six areas of specialization on their vitae were judged incompetent in at least two. This created a "Catch–22" dilemma—the committee had no knowledge concerning which were the applicant's two areas of "incompetence." As the committee chair claimed, "It's like playing Russian roulette with a six-shooter that has two bullets. We're better off sending these people 'don't call us, we'll call you' letters than risking hiring someone who's incompetent in a crucial area."

Since becoming a professor at a small midwestern college, I've encountered colleagues who teach as many as twelve different courses every two academic years (six per year). The admittedly rigorous "four areas of specialization rule" suggests these faculty and their students are routinely playing Russian roulette with a twelve shooter that has eight bullets. Although this is an extreme example, unwieldy and diverse teaching loads are common in most small colleges, making it inevitable that instructors will occasionally teach courses outside their primary areas of expertise. This paper offers some recommendations which will help faculty to cope with this problem while maintaining a pretense of sanity (and perhaps a shred of integrity).

SHORING-UP BEFORE SHIPPING-OUT:
RECOMMENDATIONS BEFORE THE SEMESTER
BEGINS

The surest antidote for ignorance is obviously knowledge. Consequently, enrolling in one or two appropriate graduate-level courses at a local university shortly before teaching a new class largely obviates the problem of incompetence. Unfortunately, competing demands for time and money make this a viable option only during sabbatical years and summer vacations.

A more practical approach is the "quick fix to competency"

technique initiated ten to twelve weeks before the new course begins. Here, three important steps are involved: (1) contacting local colleagues, (2) building a library of texts and reference works, and (3) contacting one's national professional assocation.

Contacting Local Colleagues

It is extremely helpful to telephone or write several colleagues in nearby small colleges who have experience teaching the course. After explaining one's predicament, ask them to send photocopies of their syllabi, reading lists, class materials, and even excerpts from their lecture notes. While this request sounds like an imposition, most professors will be secretly flattered—the perception that they are aiding a "struggling" colleague brings with it an ego-boosting feeling of intellectual superiority (see Goode, 1967).

Building a Library of Texts and Reference Works

A fairly complete list of relevant texts, anthologies, and reference works can be swiftly compiled by consulting recent journal advertisements and book reviews. Numerous examination copies can then be requested from the list. It is useful to skim as many of these books as possible before the course begins and again later when searching for lecture material.

Contacting One's National Professional Association

Most national professional associations now offer memberships in specific teaching sections/subdivisions and publish many pertinent materials. For example, the American Sociological Association contains a section devoted to undergraduate education, sponsors numerous workshops on teaching and curriculum issues (through the "ASA Projects on Teaching Undergraduate Sociology"), publishes a journal (*Teaching Sociology*), and distributes teaching materials (through the "ASA Teaching Resources Center"). In particular, the ASA Teaching Resources Center offers a myriad of useful items (including invaluable teaching handbooks containing model syllabi, classroom materials, teaching tips, annotated bibliographies of text-books and articles, and model exercises and assignments), com-piled for most areas in sociology. A telephone inquiry to any major national professional association will uncover similar resources for the instructor new to an area.

KEEPING AFLOAT WHILE MIDSTREAM: RECOMMENDATIONS WHILE THE COURSE IS IN PROGRESS

After the semester begins, conflicting demands for time and energy make it difficult to compensate for insufficient exper-tise. Still, five measures can be taken to enhance student impressions of competence: (1) honesty without disclosure, (2) careful selection of lecture materials, (3) liberal use of nonlec-ture resources, (4) organization and preparation, and (5) in-terest and enthusiasm.

Honesty Without Disclosure

Students paying $150 per credit hour don't want to hear instructors on the first day of class say: "I've never taught this course before, so we're going to learn it together" or "I haven't read anything on this topic since my sophomore year in college, which means I'm fairly rusty." Persistent self-effacing com-ments regarding expertise can cause students to judge even knowledgeable instructors incompetent. Neither should the in-structor new to an area claim expertise not actually possessed—brighter students are extremely adept at detecting and expos-ing a charlatan (which sometimes causes the instructor to lose credibility with an entire class; see Eble, 1972). Perhaps the best policy is to say nothing about expertise when you suspect you possess little—ignorance is not bliss but silence regarding ignorance may be golden. When cornered by difficult student questions, however, the professor must be willing occasionally to admit "I don't know." The alternative may be to heap fab-rication and obfuscation on error, necessitating, in Eble's words, "leav[ing] town with no forwarding address"(1976:130).

Careful Selection of Lecture Materials

Because textbook materials are usually well organized and competently presented, lectures based on texts are generally reasonably effective. Still, most students resent being spoon-fed lectures from their own texts (Goldsmid and Wilson, 1980). As a result, it is essential for the professor teaching outside his or her expertise to write lectures using other course-related texts than the one(s) required in class. Also, the more texts used for lectures the better—too often, reliance on one or two texts causes course presentations to be conspicuously slanted or superficial. In contrast, a comparison of several texts enables the instructor to gain a relatively comprehensive grasp of the pivotal issues in a new area and provides a wider selection of classroom examples.

Furthermore, it is helpful for the instructor to "bend" lecture materials in a new course in the direction of his or her strengths. For example, the sociologist mostly proficient in criminology will more competently teach a marriage and family course by emphasizing such topics as domestic violence and the legal aspects of marriage and the family. In most circumstances, students probably evaluate narrow competence more favorably than broad incompetence.

Whenever possible, it is also a good idea to begin preparing lecture material well in advance of the day it will be used. More diligent students are occasionally several days ahead in their readings and hence may raise embarrassing questions for unsuspecting and unprepared instructors.

Liberal Use of Nonlecture Resources

Audiovisual materials, field trips, and guest speakers usefully stretch a meager supply of lectures. Especially when used in conjunction with instructor commentary, these techniques also seem to facilitate effective learning (McKeachie, 1969). Unfortunately, professors teaching outside their expertise rarely know where to locate relevant films and resource persons. Here again, contacts with a national professional association and local colleagues are indispensable (the former can provide information concerning nationally distributed audiovisual materials; the latter can offer helpful recommendations for films and area resource persons or organizations).

Student presentation assignments (including literature reviews, reports on term papers, or summaries of chapters from texts and/or anthologies) and student-oriented class discussions (including student debates, small group "buzz" sessions, panel discussions, and role-playing sequences) can also help supplement lectures (for an excellent review of the relative merits of these techniques, see McKeachie, 1969). In this circumstance, what is good for the professor may be good for the student—research suggests that students often benefit more from class discussions than lectures (see McKeachie, 1969; Goldsmid and Wilson, 1980). For example, Goldsmid and Wilson's review of the social sciences teaching literature reveals that discussion formats are just as effective as lectures

in teaching factual information, possibly more effective in changing attitudes toward subject matter and motivating students for continued study, and more effective in teaching higher cognitive skills, such as problem solving, application, and synthesis. (1980:281)

When using student-centered assignments and discussions, however, it is still important for the instructor to continue to structure and channel classroom activities—empirical evidence indicates that achievement of knowledge objectives in a discussion is positively correlated with the degree of instructor supervision (McKeachie, 1969).

Organization and Preparation

Skillful organization and preparation—cleverly disguised by an improvisational delivery—can do much to conceal an instructor's inadequacies in expertise. In this regard, such mundane strategies as clearly specifying course objectives and requirements, writing well-structured lecture notes, and using lecture outlines on overhead projector transparencies or a chalkboard can enhance both student perceptions of instructor competence and learning (McKeachie, 1969). Research shows that organization variables (including clarity of presentation and daily class preparation) are more strongly related to favorable student evaluations of teaching than student perceptions of instructor knowledgeability (Friedrich and Michalak, 1983). Students occasionally suffer fools gladly, but rarely disorganized fools.

Interest and Enthusiasm

Effective teaching not only requires organization and preparation but also interest and enthusiasm on the part of the instructor (Eble, 1972). Unfortunately, enthusiasm can be a rare commodity when teaching a course outside one's expertise—after all, if the instructor were really excited about the topic, he or she probably would have taken courses on it in graduate school. However, even if a professor doesn't care for the subject matter in a particular course, professional integrity demands caring for students. Interest in students and the learning process should unquestionably transcend disinterest in subject matter as a motivating force for effective teaching.

Eble (1972) contends that enthusiasm for teaching emerges from many other sources besides knowledge—or even liking—of subject matter. For example, sensitivity, compassion, and devotion toward students, the thrill of the "quick-witted" intellectual exchange, and appreciation for intentional (and sometimes unintentional) classroom humor all make teaching a rewarding experience (Eble, 1972). An instructor who knows and cares little about a particular course still can enthusiastically meet the daily demands of preparation and lecturing by savoring these multifaceted "smaller" classroom pleasures.

SOME ETHICAL CONSOLATIONS AND EXPERTISE CONDOLENCES

Even if the instructor successfully dodges immediate disaster when teaching a course outside his or her areas of specialization, lingering doubts regarding propriety remain. Is it ethical to teach a course when one's "expertise" in the area is merely a consequence of the fact one is one chapter ahead of the students in the assigned reading? In this situation, aren't students and parents cheated when the bursar accepts payment for their tuition fees? More fundamentally, aren't we denying students an education and by extension jeopardizing their futures?

Some empirical evidence on student evaluations of teaching and student acquisition of knowledge offers surprising answers for these questions. For example, Feldman's (1976) review of numerous studies indicates that "knowledge of subject matter" is only one of eight factors students attribute to superior teachers (the other seven are "stimulation of interest," "clarity," "preparation," "enthusiasm," "helpfulness," "friendliness," and "openness to other's opinions"). Instructors weak on subject matter can salvage good student evaluations by displaying the other teaching virtues.

More importantly, Friedrich and Michalak's (1983) research reveals that instructor knowledgeability is not the only attribute associated with student learning. Two equally important characteristics are "organization" (including the instructor's clarity of presentation and daily preparation) and "challenge" (including the degree of difficulty of the course and the extent to which the instructor "intellectually challenges" the students). As a result, *the organized, rigorous instructor teaching outside his or her areas of expertise is not shortchanging students* (if only because such an instructor typically works long hours to compensate for academic deficiencies).

In the final analysis, diligent small college professors shortchange only themselves when teaching outside their expertise. Limitations on time and other resources mean the struggle to achieve marginal proficiency in a new academic area may result in the loss of real expertise and currency in an old area. After teaching in a small college for many years, some professors may feel trapped in a nether world between competence and incompetence in many courses. Ironically, small college professors who start their careers by successfully concealing they have no clothes in two or three courses run the risk of finishing their careers with no academic regalia whatsoever.

8

Front Burner or Back? Making Room for Research at the Small College

JAN P. VERMEER

Few college faculty members learned how to teach in graduate school. In contrast to teachers at the secondary or elementary levels, training of future college professors is centered almost exclusively on subject matter (McCulloch, 1979). If my experience was typical, graduate students do not bother very much with developing teaching styles; in fact, the notion of teaching style itself is foreign. And graduate students rarely pay much attention to the techniques their instructors used in the classes they attended. Although most plan to spend their careers sharing knowledge with new generations of students, the emphasis in graduate school is on knowledge, not on sharing.

Although the early stages of graduate careers emphasize learning about the chosen discipline, later stages involve more and more sophisticated research. The professor-to-be progresses from term papers and literature reviews to research notes, original research designs, and eventually the dissertation. Striving to become full-fledged professionals in the field, graduate students focus their energies and attention on increasingly specialized and esoteric topics. And for most, the research itself is challenging and rewarding; it turns out to be an appealing and comfortable niche.

Those students who take positions at research-oriented universities find it possible to continue their immersion in their chosen specialties. Their teaching loads are relatively light (in comparison to the loads at small liberal arts colleges) and, with the exception of occasional turns at large introductory sections, their assignments fall exclusively within their acknowledged areas of expertise. Not only are they expected to continue their research, but their teaching loads and assignments complement those efforts.

Not so for faculty at small colleges. We have heavy teaching loads—I've had at least three different preparations (and usually four) each semester I've taught for the last ten years, and always four courses per semester. We must teach outside our admitted areas of competence (expertise is too high an expectation)—I've taught courses in fields where I've never taken a course. And we must spread ourselves rather thinly among those courses and preparations, receiving only minimal aid from student graders, assistants, or secretaries. Teaching is frequently excellent; it is research that suffers.

Yet even small colleges reward significant research results. The signals small college administrators send faculty may be inconsistent (see Rich and Jolicoeur, 1978), and I'm unconvinced that all schools adequately reward substantial research efforts or that all small college administrations go out of their way to accommodate those of us with research interests. Yet professors who present papers at professional meetings, write chapters for books, publish articles in professional journals, write book reviews, and/or publish books earn respect, even in the small college environment. These professors are more likely, I suspect, to be promoted and receive raises, and their opinions are frequently sought when school-wide issues are considered.

But teaching is the main concern of small colleges, teaching undergraduates who are frequently uninterested in research and whose own term papers rarely infect the faculty member with the research bug. And because small college faculty have heavy teaching loads, they respond to the institutional mission and devote their main efforts to effective and competent teaching. They put their research interests on the back burner and plan for the time when they can pursue them—the too infrequent sabbatical year or the too-short summer.

The thought is well-intentioned but misguided. Although teaching undergraduates may be the main mission of the institution, it does not follow that it must therefore be the chief or only preoccupation of its faculty. Research should not be placed on the back burner. Graduate school training is not, as I mentioned before, in teaching—it is in research, and it is a great mistake for small college faculty to forget this fact. The goal must be to use faculty talents so that both the institutional mission—effective teaching—and the faculty's professional interests are cultivated and mutually nurtured.

I present here several sets of ideas that can help my colleagues at small colleges combine the demands of a heavy teaching load with effective and substantial research. And, of course, I am writing most directly to those small college faculty members who want to maintain a research agenda (my impression is that most faculty are unlikely to feel satisfied at a small college without being involved in active research). Even when research does not produce publishable results, it is worth the effort because it helps faculty to fulfill expectations about themselves that have been nurtured since graduate school. Many of the suggestions that follow also have the valuable by-product of actually improving teaching, a result the administration will welcome and applaud.

THE RESEARCH TOPIC

Most scholars have some research ideas. Unfortunately, most of those that immediately come to mind are unlikely candidates for serious work. The main reason for this is that most topics are not the kind that one can handle while teaching full-time at a small, liberal arts college. But at the same time, many other topics could readily be developed into appropriate research endeavors. Research topics should not simply be discarded because they require too much work for the available time. Instead, some rethinking of the choice of research topic should be undertaken. Here is what is involved.

The topic must be an area where one is relatively well versed with the literature. Now, my interests generally tend to lie where I've done substantial reading (in fact, the relationship is probably reversed: I have done substantial reading where my interests lie). But it is a fact of small college academic life that faculty members do not have the time to develop expertise in areas in which they have done little work. One must begin by building on one's own strength, just as good research builds on the work done by previous scholars. Most professors have one or two areas such as I'm describing—they need only catch up with relatively recent developments (from the last five to ten years). Start here—read a journal article a week in the field. Surprisingly quickly, one will be substantially up-to-date.

The reading may suggest a number of topics or projects. The traditional advice for students is applicable: break the project down into manageable components. If the goal is ultimately a book, do not tackle the project as a book-length endeavor. Instead, write a series of papers developing a common theme from a variety of angles. Each paper becomes the aim, providing a focus for research activity. This creates stopping points, short-term goals, and a sense of both accomplishment and satisfaction.

THE RESEARCH DATA

As much as possible, use easily accessible data. Colleagues at major research institutions will find it convenient to use data banks or archives, but few small colleges can afford to pay the required access fees for using, for example, the Inter-University Consortium for Political and Social Research. Small college faculty cannot compete with researchers at large schools who monopolize these data. Consequently, the small college researcher needs to use alternate sources of information. Aggregate rather than survey data, local literary archives rather than national document collections, census reports rather than participant observation, and replications of national studies at the local level come to mind as possible fruitful ways of proceeding.

INCORPORATING RESEARCH INTO TEACHING

The constructive introduction of research into teaching yields great benefits. At least once a semester, probably in no more than one course, a faculty member should present a lecture based on his or her current research. It might be a session of an introductory class—in my case, American government—or it might be in an advanced class, where students can be expected to be more aware of the intricacies of research. But in either case, two favorable developments are likely to ensue. First, in preparing for the class session, the researcher/professor is forced to summarize neatly his or her major research arguments. Second, this approach incorporates research tasks into class preparation, reducing the guilt about pursuing research when the instructor must face three classes the next day.

Of course, it helps tremendously to adopt an even more comprehensive research orientation in one's courses. Small colleges frequently have upper-level enrollments which facilitate seminar formats. Where this is the case, student research efforts remind the faculty member constantly of his or her own research concerns, a gentle but continual prod to continue one's own work.

The basic orientation that helps most is unabashedly and unapologetically to focus the course structure on the aspect of the field most congenial to the instructor's research interests. No doubt only one advanced course per semester, perhaps per year, is amenable to this treatment, but the biggest drawback to instructors adopting this approach is that they may believe their students would be shortchanged. This belief is sincere but mistaken. A good course always has an emphasis, and a course organized around an instructor's research interests has a theme which the faculty member can teach as an expert (rather than a theme with which he or she is familiar only through the research of others). A course organized around the professor's research interests makes the most of an instructor's expertise.

Why not take advantage of our authority as instructors? I'm not advocating abusing power by forcing students to do our research for us, but rather taking advantage of the opportunities to develop the parallels between the assignments given students and the research tasks we would like to undertake. The obvious option is to design a seminar around one's own research, as graduate-level seminars are sometimes conducted. Small college faculty will probably have few chances to go this far, and even when the opportunity is at hand, they may not attract the caliber of students necessary to make the enterprise a success. Professors fortunate enough to find themselves in a situation where a research seminar will work should take advantage of it and thank their lucky stars.

But other assignments may be more workable and helpful. Take for example the standard term paper. It is quite feasible to introduce students to the task by teaching them to prepare a bibliography. The first step in any research project, whether advanced or beginning, is to discover the fruits of previous work. So why not give students bibliographic assignments which coincide with the instructor's research interests? One of my areas of interest, for example, is congressional elections, and I have occasionally found the bibliographies prepared by my students helpful in keeping me aware of articles and journals I rarely run across. Yet because I know about many of the major papers in the field, I also can evaluate their bibliographies with much greater assurance. Consequently, the assignment benefits them as well as me.

Even more useful is preparing exercises from one's own data sets for class use. I have to admit that I am just beginning to do this, but the prospect is challenging. Instructors frequently rely on examples to illustrate the principles with which they are concerned. If those principles can be demonstrated by the evidence the professor has collected in his or her own research, this can be made available in an appropriate format for students. Several political scientists at Providence College have gone so far as to start their own data center (Trudeau, Hyde, and Carlson, 1982). Quantitative data can help illustrate simple statistical principles; both quantitative and qualitative evidence can help illustrate various points in class contexts. There are two reasons why student attempts to analyze the same data the instructor is concerned with augment research tremendously. First, the need to explain to students what the data set contains, how it can be used to evaluate hypotheses, and what kinds of conclusions the evidence supports keeps the instructor actively involved in data analysis. Sometimes students will come up with surprising conclusions, some of which will provide helpful insights, and others of which will tax the instructor's ingenuity in convincing the students that their interpretations are inaccurate. In either case, faculty members are deeply and significantly involved in the analysis of their evidence. Second, using one's own research data as teaching material enables instructors to resolve the conflict between devoting time to teaching and spending energies on research. This teaching strategy allows one to do research in order to make teaching more effective. Of course, a professor's draft essay on a philosophical or literary topic can serve a similar purpose in humanities classes.

A NOTE ON BUDGETING TIME

Time constraints still loom as a major problem for small college faculty pursuing research; when several daily preparations stare an instructor in the face, teaching deadlines often crowd out other work. The answer is to reassert control over one's schedule. Every week, an instructor should try to set aside four hours (preferably in one block) for research. What's important is not so much how the time is used—library research, laboratory experiments, or writing—but that the time is set aside and considered as sacrosanct as time allocated for committee meetings and lunch breaks. This may mean negotiations with department chairs and colleagues about course meeting times, and it may occasionally mean teaching two courses in succession, but without preserving large blocks of time, conducting research is virtually impossible. Few of us can do enough in the evenings and on weekends to make progress, given the not unwarranted demands of family, friends, church, and community for our participation.

COLLABORATION

Collaboration is another useful way for the professor in the small college to pursue research. Solitary research endeavors may bring renown and a glorious reputation, but working with another researcher creates its own pleasures and rewards. As Fox and Faven (1984:350) suggest, "collaboration and colleagueship are particularly important for scholars . . . who have heavy teaching appointments." Let me illustrate several ways cooperative research helps overcome the barriers small college faculty face in trying to conduct credible research.

First, working with another researcher gives one an obligation to fulfill (Fox and Faven, 1984). It is no longer easy to postpone research efforts; after all, someone else is waiting for a contribution to the joint project. A commitment to work jointly with someone else becomes a commitment that is more difficult to break than a promise to oneself to work on a project "just as soon as I get these papers graded." Especially if the collaborators meet regularly, one has incremental deadlines to meet. There is no reason to limit one's choice of collaborators to other faculty; significant work can build on the contributions of students. For example, in political science, the famous Kelley, Ayres, and Bowen (1967) research project on registration and voting developed out of a senior thesis by Ayres.

Second, collaboration allows the two researchers to complement each other's special areas of expertise. The media specialist and the campaigning scholar can work together on communication strategies by local election challengers, a task neither could perhaps do alone without the kind of substantial background reading and study that teaching in the small college doesn't permit. Especially fruitful is cross-disciplinary research with colleagues at the same school. The sociologist, historian, political scientist, economist, and anthropologist have society as a common subject matter; research projects approached from two of these divergent perspectives can create fresh insights.

Third, and probably as important as any of the others, collaboration breaks the isolation that faculty at small colleges often feel. Few impediments to research are as great as the feeling that one is the only scholar who has any interest in the topic under investigation. Frequent feedback from a collaborator helps integrate the lone economist at a teaching college into the scholarly community. It provides a frame of reference, an identity, and a motivation for research (Fox and Faven, 1984). I don't mean to denigrate the value of routine interaction with fellow faculty in other disciplines, but certainly the regular, constructive, and reinforcing response from a research collaborator transcends colleague gossip about students and faculty politics.

Finally, collaboration is likely to be productive (Fox and Faven, 1984). Often, one partner knows about conferences and journals for sharing results with which the other partner is only vaguely familiar. Each partner is likely to have his or her own motivations for developing the research, which may result in one project being presented in two different ways for different audiences. Each partner is likely to be able to call upon other acquaintances and contacts for criticism of ongoing work. The final product can only benefit as a result.

CONCLUSION

I am not suggesting that combining a heavy teaching load with research commitments is easy. Nor am I arguing that more effective teaching will automatically result from greater research efforts—the verdict is still out on this issue, although some recent research suggests there is little direct connection between research participation and student evaluations of teaching competence (Friedrich and Michalak, 1983). But Friedrich and Michalak's research results also

deny the common complaint that there is not enough time to be a good researcher and a good teacher; they indicate that it is possible to do good research without detracting significantly from the time and attention devoted to teaching. And they suggest the key to reconciling the demands of the two: organization. (1983:160)

The small college faculty member who wants to do research can. It takes planning, hard work, organization, and determination, but the results can be teaching energized by current professional concerns. It is important to remember that research can be done without sacrificing teaching effectiveness. In fact, faculty members may gain student respect as researhers in touch with their fields. It is true that keeping up with the latest developments in one's discipline is difficult, but it is a delusion to think that students don't notice to what extent instructors are current. Substantial research efforts help—the personal pursuit of research forces faculty to do more than merely skim the latest textbooks for new ideas, concepts, and theories.

In addition, as a productive scholar in his or her discipline, the small college professor can readily relate class materials to current debates in the field. The faculty member is apt to demonstrate an enthusiasm for the subject matter which goes well beyond teaching—enthusiasm which reflects an enjoyment of the subject demonstrated by the personal pursuit of knowledge in the field. Ancient lecture examples surviving from classes the instructor took as a graduate student would begin to be replaced by more pertinent ones from the teacher's own scholarly endeavors.

Small college administrators can only be pleased by these developments. Scholarly articles and conference papers are customarily presented with the institutional affiliation of the author clearly indicated. As the visibility of the institution grows, prestige follows, and the president of the school has further ammunition to use in his or her quest for funds from foundations and alumni.

Small college faculty should respect research efforts. They should not turn their backs on their graduate school training or on their substantive interests because they believe it is impossible to combine effective teaching at a small college with substantial and significant research. It is a question of making—not finding—the time and manipulating the context within which one works to one's advantage. The rewards are there: professional and personal for the research itself, and institutional for the recognition from students and administrators. Research on the back burner provides no satisfaction and offers no reward. It should be moved to the front burner!

9

A Case Study of a Cooperative Department Among Several Small Colleges

RICHARD S. REMPEL

Many of us choose to teach at a small college for personal reasons—a denominational tie, a cultural heritage, or an academic program that has a unique attraction. The size of the small college also offers some inducements, such as greater opportunities to play a major role in shaping the academic program and to know students more closely. However, there are unquestionably some major disadvantages to teaching at such a school. These include limitations in breadth of program, the need for each instructor to teach many different courses, the likelihood of having to do the administrative duties of running a department, and a lack of colleagues with whom to share professional and disciplinary interest (see Flanders, 1971).

Establishing cooperative departments among several colleges is one way to keep the advantages while ameliorating the disadvantages of small colleges. This chapter describes a cooperative mathematical sciences department, reviewing its strengths and weaknesses and the factors that contribute to those strengths and weaknesses.

CONTEXT AND EARLY HISTORY

Bethel, McPherson, and Tabor colleges in central Kansas lie on an approximately equilateral triangle with sides of about

25 miles each. Bethel is related to the General Conference Mennonite church and has about 640 students and 55 fulltime faculty. McPherson is related to the Church of the Brethren and has about 470 students and 30 fulltime faculty. Tabor is related to the Mennonite Brethren church and has about 440 students and 27 fulltime faculty.

All three colleges are members of the Associated Colleges of Central Kansas (henceforth referred to as ACCK), a consortium that also includes Bethany and Sterling colleges and Kansas Wesleyan University. The larger consortium, formed in 1966, features a common 4–1–4 calendar and a central office with a minicomputer which has been used for administrative and academic purposes by all the consortium colleges. ACCK conducts a computer science program, secondary methods courses for prospective high school teachers in various disciplines, and a special education program in which most member colleges participate. There is also a courier service which distributes library materials and mail among the campuses four times a week. There is an annual ACCK meeting at which faculty members meet by discipline, and some discipline committees have collaborated on projects such as off-campus tours during the January interterm. From the beginning of the consortium, the Mathematics Committee cooperatively offered joint courses during the interterms and occasionally brought in visiting lecturers.

This cooperation led to other joint ventures. Bethel College mathematics faculty taught courses at both McPherson and Tabor colleges, because Bethel's department had two faculty members while the other departments each had one. In the fall of 1972, Professor Arnold M. Wedel, chairperson of the Mathematics Department at Bethel, suggested to William Keeney, provost of the college, that this cooperative arrangement be regularized. Keeney pursued discussions with the deans of McPherson and Tabor, along with the dean at Hesston College (a two-year school operated by the Mennonite church and situated eight miles from Bethel). After a series of meetings by the deans and mathematics faculty of the four colleges during the spring of 1973, the following agreements were accepted:

1. Mathematics personnel from the four schools would form a cooperative department, charged with teaching all mathematics and several related courses (e.g., computer science and secondary school mathematics methods) at the colleges.

2. The department would develop a common curriculum meeting the needs of the participating colleges, with the primary curriculum objective to maximize quality and efficiency without any anticipated program expansion. Most upper-level and some lower-level courses would be taught cooperatively. Students (and also often instructors) would drive from the other colleges to the campuses on which the cooperative courses were to be taught.

3. Central College of McPherson (a two-year school operated by the Free Methodist church) would also be invited to participate on the same basis as Hesston. Different financial arrangements were adopted for the two-year colleges.

4. New mathematics personnel at any participating institution would be hired in consultation with the other schools to try to insure compatability with the continuing program commitments.

5. The cooperative arrangement was not intended in any way to diminish the participation of the Bethel, McPherson, or Tabor Mathematical Sciences departments in the larger ACCK consortium. The other ACCK institutions were to be kept fully informed of all cooperative department developments.

A proposal to finance some of the planning and coordination costs involved in the creation of the cooperative department was submitted to the Hesston Foundation and was funded for a total of $7,500 for the 1973–74 and 1974–75 academic years.

CURRENT ORGANIZATION

The cooperative department has continued to operate and develop on the basis of the original agreement. Two major structural changes have occurred since 1973. First, the two-year colleges have withdrawn from formal membership in the department, although they still cooperate on a course-by-course basis. Second, the size of the computer science program within the department has grown rapidly. In the late 1960s, the only computer science courses available to our students were the two or three courses per semester offered by ACCK and taught at McPherson (which is in the center of the larger six-college consortium). By 1973, when our cooperative department was formed, most colleges had their own sections of one course— Introduction to Computer Science. This was soon followed by sections of other programming language courses, such as FOR-TRAN and COBOL. Now each campus offers a full complement of lower-level programming courses, and the next level of computer science courses is being developed. ACCK continues to offer upper-level computer science courses when enrollments are too small to justify sections on the individual campuses. By now the computer science program within the cooperative department almost rivals the mathematics program in size. The programs remain combined under the name "mathematical sciences," reflecting the philosophy that these areas (along with statistics and operations research) are strengthened by remaining in a close relationship.

In the 1983–84 academic year, 24 different courses (totaling 89 credit hours) were made available in the mathematical sciences to all Bethel, McPherson, and Tabor students. This total does not count independent studies, seminars, topic courses, and practicums, some of which were conducted on each campus. There was a total of 54 sections of the 24 different courses offered, with Bethel, McPherson, and Tabor paying for 50 and ACCK paying for 4. This meant the money a college paid for approximately 17 sections bought the opportunity for its students to choose from 24 courses. The number of sections varied from one each for twelve courses (most of which were cooperatively offered) to nine for variations of the computer literacy course. The sections can be classified as follows: nine sections of the calculus sequence; six sections of precalculus; eight sections of lower-level mathematics service courses; five sections of various upper-level mathematics courses; nine sections of computer literacy courses; seven sections of the introductory programming sequence; five sections of computer science service courses; and five sections of upper-level computer science.

Eight upper-level mathematics courses are regularly offered by the department—four or five each year on an every-other-year schedule. Advanced analysis, modern geometry, applied mathematics, operations research, and mathematical statistics are taught one year; and modern algebra, combinatorics and graph theory, applied mathematics, and probability the next. In addition, arranged courses are offered on topics in algebra and analysis.

Two upper-level courses taught in the spring semester 1984 illustrate the efficiency which a cooperative department provides. Operations research had an enrollment of seventeen: five from Bethel, six from McPherson, and six from Tabor. Applied mathematics for the physical sciences had an enrollment of ten: four from Bethel, four from McPherson, and two from Tabor. Combining enrollments enabled both classes to be financially acceptable to administrators while fostering a high-quality classroom atmosphere for students. Without cooperation each college would have had to choose between offering both courses—a decision difficult to justify financially—or offering at most one, limiting student educational opportunities.

We are proud of the quality of our program. Our combined resources allow us to provide students with a breadth and level of preparation well suited for graduate school or first jobs. Our graduates have created a solid record of achievement in graduate schools and in their careers. For example, all three colleges have mathematical sciences graduates who have finished or are currently finishing Ph.D. programs at major universities.

ADVANTAGES FOR THE COLLEGES

As can be seen, a cooperative department can provide participating colleges with the opportunity to offer a more complete program with considerable financial efficiency. Another advantage is the ability to increase or decrease personnel and courses without a serious financial impact on any college—one new person can be added to the cooperative department at an average cost of one-third person to each participating school. While the mathematics portion of our department has made significant curriculum changes, faculty size has remained almost constant. In contrast, the computer science program has grown from no full-time faculty in 1972 to more than one faculty position per campus (with more growth likely in the near future). The ability to hire faculty as needed while sharing costs and teaching loads among the three campuses has facilitated orderly growth in computer science.

In recent years it has been very difficult for colleges and universities to find qualified computer science faculty. This is a particularly serious problem for small colleges, considering their limited equipment and programs and poor salaries. To make matters worse, small college administrators may want to hire one person to teach upper-level computer science courses, computer literacy courses for nonmajors, and service courses for business students. Our cooperative department, however, has met all three needs on each campus by hiring three instructors (one at each college), each of whom has the qualifications and interests to do an excellent job in one or two of the three areas.

ADVANTAGES FOR STUDENTS AND FACULTY

One advantage to students of a cooperative department is the opportunity for exposure to more faculty (and hence a wider variety of approaches and styles of instruction). A corresponding disadvantage is that faculty members from other campuses are not as available for student appointments.

The faculty member teaching a lower-level or service course on another campus seems especially vulnerable to student criticism. However, such problems can be minimized through firm and vocal administrative and departmental support at the local campus. For lower-level courses, the provision of a local student assistant who is available to tutor students in the class is invaluable. If the student assistant is carefully chosen, many of the potential problems can be dealt with satisfactorily. We have also worked to assure that each instructor maintains regular office hours on the campus where the course is taught.

A cooperative department provides several benefits to faculty members. One is the opportunity to teach in one's area of expertise and interest. Another is the opportunity for more collegiality than is normally possible in a one- or two-person department. Our cooperative department tries to provide occasions for interaction among members in a variety of ways.

We hold monthly departmental meetings over Saturday breakfast (these sessions provide an excellent opportunity for informal discussion of a variety of issues on a continuing basis). The combined resources in our cooperative department have also enabled us to bring in outside speakers of national and even international prominence.

Beginning in 1975, the cooperative department has conducted annual spring seminars (see Bailie and Hall, 1975). Topics have ranged widely in pure and applied mathematics, and have included discussions of mathematical models of conflict and peace, algebraic number theory, mathematical economics, logic, mathematical biology, uses of mathematics in industry, algebraic topology, group representation theory, and a colloquim on Douglas R. Hofstadter's *Godel, Escher, Bach: An Eternal Golden Braid* (1979). The spring seminars have been organized by resource people from our own cooperative department, other departments in our colleges, and graduates of our colleges.

TRAVEL AND SCHEDULES

Travel is one obvious problem in a cooperative department among noncontiguous campuses. A 1978–79 survey of all travel by faculty members among the campuses indicated an estimated total of 14,160 miles. A majority of these trips included students riding with faculty to classes. Whenever possible, however, schedules are arranged to minimize travel. For example, two cooperative courses offered the same semester may be scheduled the same hours on the same campus, so that students and faculty from the other two campuses can drive together. The location of a class is chosen whenever possible to minimize the number of people who must travel to it.

At times college vehicles are used for travel. For several years the department had the use of an older car donated by a faculty member. But usually department members and/or students have to use their own vehicles. This has at times been a burden, even though some travel reimbursement has been provided by the participating colleges.

Another aspect of the travel problem is time and scheduling.

Instructors and students must plan a 30- to 40-minute cushion around each cooperative course held on another campus. This adds up to a significant amount of time over the course of a semester and makes scheduling of cooperative classes difficult. We try to deal with the scheduling problem by relying on pre-determined times for as many cooperative classes as possible, both for scheduling and transportation convenience. Once travel becomes a fact of life for mathematics majors, it is reasonably well accepted, and does not seem to be a significant barrier to majoring in mathematics.

CONCLUSION: REQUIREMENTS FOR SUCCESS

In summary, the benefits of developing a cooperative department among several small colleges include a more complete program and more flexibility of curriculum and staffing. Students are exposed to a wider variety of courses and of faculty expertise, styles, and approaches. Faculty members have better opportunities for collegiality and professional development. Most of the problems for students and faculty are related to the need to travel among campuses.

Clearly the chief requirement for success of a cooperative department is commitment to cooperation by the college administrators and the department members. In our case, the 1973 agreement has remained strong and effective due to such commitment. At the same time, similar cooperative arrangements between Bethel and Hesston colleges have failed. The attitudes of these two colleges toward cooperation could be characterized as interest without commitment. The result is that cooperative arrangements survive only until a change in personnel occurs in one of the participating departments. This suggests that if a college is strongly committed to the success of a cooperative department, it must include a commitment to cooperation as a part of the job description for prospective department members. There must be a philosophy that longer-term cooperation is too important to be sacrificed for short-term gain or convenience.

Commitment by faculty members to a cooperative program is most likely to arise through friendships with colleagues in the other institutions. Where friendship is the sole basis for commitment, however, cooperation may not survive personnel changes. A more lasting basis for faculty commitment to cooperation is a desire for professional involvement in one's discipline. A cooperative department provides colleagues who can collaborate in research or other areas of professional development, help with teaching problems, and advise on problems relating to faculty politics.

The long record of success of the cooperative department described here suggests that it should be considered as a model for cooperative departments elsewhere. What are the conditions in which cooperative departments could flourish? One obvious requirement is geographical proximity. A second important consideration is a compatibility of program goals and quality among the colleges and their student bodies. Another consideration is size of the constituent departments. Departments with fewer than four faculty and those with needs for half-time positions are the most likely candidates to find major advantages in cooperation. Some disciplines may have more difficulty in cooperating due to special laboratory needs. But the chief ingredient for success is the desire to make it work. If such a desire is present, a cooperative department can provide significant benefits to students, faculty, and administrators.

10

The Dual Role of the Physical Educator—Coach: Problems and Solutions for Small Colleges

PAUL N. GRABER

A HISTORICAL OVERVIEW AND RECENT CHANGES

At the turn of the century, major American universities—faced with expanding athletic programs—began to separate athletics from academia (Rudolph, 1962). The eventual result was "big time" athletic programs with budgets climbing into the millions of dollars (Henschen, 1977). At about the same time, diverse systems of gymnastics and the English system of sport were combined and modified to form the present-day field of physical education.

At major universities today, athletics have been separated from academia creating a "double standard." On the one hand, the faculty member with a Ph.D. degree, several years of successful teaching experience in physical education, and an acceptable publication record teaches full-time physical education in a "publish or perish" environment. On the other hand, the physical-education trained person with a master's degree and usually intercollegiate playing experience coaches in a "win or perish" athletic department, while earning a considerably higher salary than the full-time physical education instructor.

The "double standard" at the major university changes to

"double duty" at the small college, where coaches are also required to teach. Without a doubt, double duty in small colleges reduces the severity of the "publish or perish" and "win or perish" doctrines. Nevertheless, because of community or self-imposed pressures, the small college physical educator–coach still feels the need for bigger and better teams and yet is also expected to teach competently in the classroom. The entire physical education program is inescapably affected by these conflicting demands—even though physical education and athletic departments often retain separate administrators, they continue to share common facilities, personnel, and problems.

In particular, three factors recently have placed considerable stress on small college physical education and athletic departments: (1) "catch-as-catch-can" pressure to win, (2) increasing interest in women's sports, and (3) inflated costs for travel and equipment.

"Catch-as-Catch-Can" Pressure to Win

In athletics, pressure to win goes hand-in-hand with competitive American social values. Consequently, there is the need to "keep up with the Joneses," which may easily create a "catch-as-catch-can" system with the end justifying the means. If a conference leader is rumored to have more dollars for athletic scholarships and/or a larger staff, the scramble to catch up begins. When certain road blocks appear to restrict the coach's efforts to keep up, rules and guidelines may be broken or stretched beyond recognition. Constant pressure is placed on the staff to work harder and on administrators to provide more dollars. Athletic directors, unable to locate money yet held accountable for the quality of various athletic programs, often find themselves in a no-win situation.

At the same time the athletic director is attempting to deal with the controversial issues surrounding small college athletics, he or she may also be the head coach of one or more sports and teaching ten or more credit hours of physical education. All too often, these competing demands must eventually have a negative effect on the quality of physical education instruction in small colleges. The pressure to keep up and win games—in part produced by the simplistic accountability of a win-lose record—consumes the time of the physical educator–coach leaving little energy for teaching classes and/or professional development.

Increasing Interest in Women's Sports

The recent addition of numerous women's sports is another stress factor for many small colleges. The expansion in women's sports was set into motion over a decade ago by federal legislation through Title IX (Resource Center on Sex Roles in Education, 1977). Before Title IX, very few small colleges maintained equitable athletic programs for men and women— the vast majority of funding was allocated to men's programs. In a consciencious attempt to comply with the new legislation, however, small colleges expanded women's programs, both in number of sports offered and costs. At the same time, men's athletic programs strived to remain strong. These conditions necessitated a significant increase in athletic budgets for program and personnel.

Inflated Costs for Travel and Equipment

The demand for budget increases in small college athletic departments came at a time when the nation's economy was enduring unprecedented long-term double-digit inflation while many small liberal arts colleges were experiencing declining enrollments. Despite the increasing cost of travel and equipment for existing programs, it seemed inappropriate for small college athletic departments—which were already costing colleges thousands of dollars annually—to request increases in staff and operating expenses (especially considering other departmental budgets were being reduced). Nevertheless, to maintain competitive programs, some budget and staff increases were made.

THE 1980s—A TIME OF RECKONING

The 1980s are a time of reckoning for small college athletic departments. The recent budget and staff expansions described above have been costly and untimely. College faculties and administrators no longer allow athletic program budget increases which are out of proportion to increases in academic budgets. This often leaves the athletic director with the difficult task of maintaining quality programs with fixed dollars that buy less and less.

It is obvious that changes in the status quo are necessary. Athletic directors can plan and negotiate the needed changes or do nothing and run the risk of losing entire programs as funding becomes more problematic. Two alternatives for change exist—small colleges can either go the way of major universities by separating and enlarging the departments of physical education and intercollegiate athletics or can reinvigorate current programs through careful planning and coordination. Of course, in an era of budget restraint, few colleges can realistically choose the former alternative.

To change the status quo is no easy task. Should we choose to keep physical education and athletic departments together, physical educators will need to develop more skills. Teaching and coaching expertise will need to be combined with business acumen, a knowledge of adaptive physical education for the handicapped, administrative abilities, familiarity with the fields of health education and sports medicine, and skill in the use of computers as teaching and coaching aids. And as we make important decisions and changes, the mission of the small college—as it relates to physical education and athletics—must be clarified.

The athletic program at the small college must continue to give young people the opportunity to gain intercollegiate-level playing experience as they actively pursue college degrees. Still, the number of intercollegiate sports offered and supported by the small college must be determined by the number of sports the college can reasonably afford. College administrators must be made fully aware of how much money it will take to provide properly for each sport. Most importantly, quantity of programs should not be substituted for quality.

Competition is the intangible which determines if an intercollegiate sport is properly provided for. Administrators should do all they can to guarantee that teams which compete with each other, in or out of a conference, have similar budgets, staffs, and recruiting dollars. This would partially control the "catch-as-catch-can" system mentioned earlier by making it more difficult for any one team to dominate a conference or region year after year. The resulting reduction in stress and work hours currently devoted to athletic recruitment would enable the physical educator—coach to give more attention to physical education teaching and professional development.

With the realistic understanding that there will always be another sport to offer and a higher skill level at which to participate, the small college must admit that it is not in "big time" athletics. Once this is understood, small colleges will stop short of the level of athletic competition and the scale of operation which exist at major universities. The difficulty is in recognizing that bigger is not necessarily better, just different. Once we admit our difference, the temptation to imitate major university athletic programs will be lessened, and we can deal effectively with the very serious problems confronting small college physical education and athletic programs.

A NEW DIRECTION

For most American small colleges declining student enrollments and financial woes mean the 1980s will present challenges more difficult than any period since the Great Depression. Some colleges will close while in others, physical education and athletic programs will be eliminated.

As we rethink and redirect the small college physical education and athletic programs to fit the 1980s better, it is imperative for the two departments to remain united. A logical plan seems to involve curtailing program expansion and developing a more efficient approach that streamlines, alters, and (when necessary) eliminates portions of existing programs. This will enable physical education and athletic programs to become highly pertinent, defensible, and affordable.

This "new direction" requires that physical educators teach first and coach second—quality teaching must not be sacrificed to achieve quality coaching. Small college administrators should demand a high-quality physical education program first and then concern themselves with competitive athletics. The plan should phase out adjunct/support staff used in key coaching positions. Instead, important coaching positions should be assigned to physical educators, with faculty members from other departments encouraged to coach minor sports or assist with major sports.

Small college athletic conferences must also change with the times. More leadership is needed from the conference level in order to ensure that member teams abide by conference rules. A commissioner given executive power and supported by the presidents of the colleges in the conference would provide each college with a more equal opportunity to win. Winning based on hard work and commitment would flourish while winning based on dollars spent would diminish.

To meet tighter budgets, it may be necessary for some sports to be dropped from the intercollegiate level and assigned a club sport or extramural status. A limited travel budget for these programs would be the only expense the college need provide. Round-robin competition could be organized for all club sports and regulated by conference officials. In addition, intramural programs could be enlarged to help compensate for any sport lost because of economic, scheduling, or related problems.

The above suggestions are offered as steps that permit the continued existence of small college athletics. The suggestions are incomplete but constructive attempts to encourage alternative thinking relating to some serious problems. There is no question that it is easier, at least for the present, to do nothing and hence endorse a status quo solution for the problems in physical education and athletic programs. However, as students become increasingly scarce and costs rise, a status quo "solution" is ill advised. Hard decisions made now may carry small college physical education and athletic programs through still darker days yet ahead.

11

Teaching the Secular on Sacred Ground: Liberal Arts and Religion in the Small Church-Related College

DONALD HATCHER

Since their beginnings in 1636, private colleges in the U.S. have tended to be at once church-related and liberal arts institutions. The original mission of church-related colleges was to spread the Christian gospel while educating ministers for the new churches which were being established on the frontier. Hence, these early colleges emphasized liberal learning not as an end in itself, but as a means for furthering Christianity. This emphasis is especially clear in the case of Harvard, where in the first 65 years, more than half the graduates became ministers (Snavley, 1955:6).

Drawing heavily on the scholastic model of education, it was believed that no better training for future ministers could be found than the study of the liberal arts. In particular, logic and rhetoric were seen as effective tools for spreading the gospel and converting nonbelievers. Beyond courses in reasoning, the original curriculum at early church-related colleges included the study of Latin, Greek, math, natural science, and literature (Snavley, 1955:6–7). While the curriculum in these colleges has changed over the years, the commitment to the union of liberal learning and religious training remains.

Today there are over 500 church-related liberal arts colleges in 46 states. Most are fairly small with an average enrollment of just over 650 students. A large majority of the students in these colleges claim to be either Christian or Jewish. It is evident the students and alumni of these schools still believe that spiritual growth and liberal learning go hand in hand.

My experience as a philosophy professor at a small church-related institution, however, has led me to question whether the marriage of the sacred and secular is quite so sanguine. From the perspective of many of my students, religious faith is the antithesis of liberal learning. As students understand it, faith demands unquestioning belief; as most academics understand it, liberal learning demands a critical attitude toward all beliefs. Given their attitude toward faith, the task of "liberally educating" students at church-related institutions is a tremendous challenge, one that I fear is all too often not adequately met.

This paper will examine from a historical perspective the nature of the current antagonism between the critical attitude essential for liberal learning and the dogmatic attitude students tend to have toward religious faith. A clear understanding of how the antagonism arose will point to certain solutions which I have found effective in my own teaching. As will be seen, however, my solutions are not without certain difficulties which affect the college as a whole.

A HISTORY OF THE PROBLEM

To understand the current problems associated with what I call "teaching the secular on sacred ground," it may be helpful to see more clearly why religion and liberal learning were thought to be not only compatible but also complimentary. Why did early religious leaders value liberal education so highly, even though this education always included the study of texts which were either "pagan" or critical of Christian beliefs? My method will be to trace briefly the historical development of education in Western culture to see how the concepts of liberal learning and religious faith have been understood by various educators.

Throughout this examination it will be possible to see how

ideas about liberal education and its relation to religious faith have lagged behind historical developments in the natural and social sciences and philosophy. The problem is that while the subject matter necessary for liberal learning has drastically changed since the 13th century, parents, trustees, and students tend to maintain rather medieval attitudes toward the nature of Christian faith. As a consequence, professors in liberal arts disciplines find themselves teaching in institutions which at least on paper appear to be modeled after the scholastic tradition where religious faith and liberal learning were thought to lead to the same conclusion—God. Naive students arrive in classes expecting to have their faiths reinforced, only to read Nietzsche, Marx, Darwin, and Freud. Teachers committed to the liberal arts ideal of the continued search for truth and the critical attitude which accompanies this search are faced with students who are convinced they already know "the Truth." Of course, these students are naturally unreceptive to ideas which might lead them to question or think critically about their beliefs.

In seeking to understand the historical relationship between religion and liberal education, two perspectives are apparent. First, there were those who thought that one must know the Divine to attain wisdom. Education was viewed as the outcome of getting in touch with the gods. Second, there were those who thought that wisdom/liberal learning enhanced religious development. Hence, while the former considered the gods to be the means to wisdom, the latter viewed wisdom as the means to the gods.

Those who thought the acquisition of all knowledge was dependent on the gods were committed to pursuing the favor of the gods to gain wisdom and power. This was especially true in ancient Greece (Medlin, 1964: 12). The Homeric myths are filled with instances of gods—such as Athena—instructing humans they favored. Likewise, Greek tragedy around the time of Plato depicts wise men as chosen and inspired by the gods. Plato (1956:18), while at times criticizing established religion, portrays the poets as gaining their wisdom through communing with the gods. Even Socrates—the supreme iconoclast—is portrayed in the "Symposium" as one who divines with the gods to attain wisdom. In that dialogue, Socrates' mentor, Diotima, has a mystical vision of the "Form of Beauty" which she communicates to Socrates (1956:72–73).

But while the early Greeks saw education and wisdom as intimately connected to religious life, Plato's later dialogues envision knowledge to be more a function of careful, critical human thought than divine revelation. With this shift in attitude, the tension between liberal education and religious faith begins. The tension is obvious when we remember that Socrates was placed on trial because the citizens of Athens believed his continued questioning of their established beliefs—the mark of a liberal education—corrupted Athenian youth (Plato, 1956:430). For the average Athenian (who believed wisdom came solely from the gods), it was only natural to see critical thought as the enemy of religious faith. And when critical thought leads Plato in his *Republic* (1956) to conclude that most of the established religious literature in the state should be censored, the apprehension by the religious leaders of the day appears understandable.

The tendency toward the separation of education and religion continues in Plato's student, Aristotle. When Aristotle writes about education, we find little to indicate that he thought it was necessary for persons to be religious to attain wisdom. Except for the description in his *Metaphysics* of the "Prime Mover" as a being involved in the activity of "thought thinking thought," there is little mention of the gods. For Aristotle, the ability to observe nature carefully and employ the tools of logical analysis, coupled with the development of the proper moral and intellectual virtues, are sufficient to lead a person to both wisdom and happiness. Aristotle sees little need to bring the gods into the educational process.

It is with Aristotle that we see the flower of classical liberal education unfolding. While Plato argues forcefully in *Republic* for the need to educate both body and soul, it is Aristotle (1941:952–59) who first develops the idea that education could shape individual dispositions. By using what is now called "positive reinforcement," Aristotle believes that desired behavioral tendencies can be imparted to the young by rewarding repeated appropriate behaviors (which causes the behavior to become what Aristotle calls "second nature"). Given this theory, Aristotle seems sure that formal education can be systematically employed to produce morally and intellectually virtuous persons. Morally virtuous people do the right thing because they are disposed to do good; intellectually virtuous people pursue wisdom because they have been taught how to do so.

While Aristotle seems to be moving toward the separation of religion and education, a change in attitudes is seen in the development of Roman education. Once Christianity was established in Rome, religious leaders begin to see liberal education in the Greek tradition as a valuable tool in furthering religion. According to William Medlin (1964:32–33):

Later Christian teachers, in both Roman and Greek parts of the Empire, were educated according to classical traditions. Tertullian, Basil the Great, John Chrysostom, Jerome, Augustine—all had read the "Great Books." They were obliged to follow the pagan (Aristotelean) ideal, both because of its social dominance and because of their vocation; to refute and interpret unacceptable classical doctrines; to educate a clergy skilled in logical and rhetorical techniques of disputation and exhortation; and to establish their new erudition in a society long accustomed to learning and scholarship.

The works of the pagans Plato and Aristotle were studied because—written prior to Christianity—they did not directly challenge Christian doctrine. Plato and Aristotle often focus their energies on the critique of existing Greek religions, which were usually polytheistic. This critique of "pagan religions" complimented the attempt of the early church to establish a logical basis for monotheism. (Ironically, as will be seen, the works of modern day Platos and Aristotles—Voltaire, Diderot, Nietzsche, and Bertrand Russell—are also critical of religious doctrine, but in this case Christianity. While Plato criticizes the less than moral behavior of the Greek pantheon and seems to be moving toward monotheism, modern thinkers tend to support either atheism or at least the deanthropomorphizing of the Christian God.)

With the Christian employment of the Greek methods of education, the function of human reason changes. While in the classical Greek tradition, the development of reason was emphasized so that humans could more adequately understand themselves and the world, medieval educators pursued reason to know and understand God. In addition, reason was seen as an effective tool for the faithful to defend their faith and show heretics where they had gone astray. Rather than criticize religion, philosophy was considered the "handmaiden of theology," and liberal learning in general was seen as a useful tool in expanding the influence of Christianity throughout the world. For example, in *Summa Theologica* (1982), Thomas Aquinas tries to show the reasonableness of believing in a Christian God and the authority of the Scriptures. Aquinas believes that if people were simply taught to observe nature (God's creation) carefully, they would be led by reason to conclude that a good, all-powerful God was surely the first cause and designer of the universe. Training in logic and the Aristotelean or teleological view of nature were considered essential for understanding this position. Ironically, what could be called the "secular humanism" of the Greeks was taught so that people's understanding of Christian wisdom could be enhanced. (Later, when the Aristotelean view of nature was replaced by Copernican and Darwinian views, the huge theological edifice built on Aristotle's philosophy also crumbled.)

During the Middle Ages, reason and critical thought were also used as powerful political instruments by the Church. According to Ellwood Cubberley (1920), the Church saw that it could not compete with the physical prowess of "barbarian" tribes. If it were to civilize barbarians, it had to do so through the force of reason and knowledge. Because reason and knowledge were thought to lead to the acceptance of the unerring authority of the Bible, it was on this authority that the Church based its power. However, after the Church's power was firmly established, there was little need for reason to go on questioning and criticizing. Once Christendom was secure, to "question, to doubt, to disbelieve—these were among the deadly sins of the early Middle Ages" (Cubberley, 1920:173).

The problem was that human reason, as understood in the classical Greek texts of Plato and Aristotle, was incompatible with dogmatism. Hence the very tool used to civilize the barbarians and to support the Church's view of the world could easily become the instrument for the demise of biblical authority. The Church, through its support of liberal education, indeed "created a monster." And when the educators of the Church realized this threat, they tried their best to destroy the very weapons they had used to win the battle. As Cubberley (1920:174, 187) notes:

Inquiry or doubt in religious matters was not tolerated, and scientific inquiry and investigation ceased to exist. The notable scientific advances of the Greeks, their literature and philosophy, and particularly their genius for free inquiry and investigation, no longer influenced a world dominated by an institution preparing its children only for life in a world to come. . . . The Christian world everywhere lay under a veil of faith, illusion, and childish prepossession. The mysteries of Christianity and the many inconsistencies of its teachings and beliefs were accepted with childlike docility.

CURRENT ANTAGONISMS

Although Cubberley is describing the Middle Ages, my experience as a philosophy professor in a small church-related college causes me to conclude that many students have not really progressed much beyond this attitude. Faith and critical inquiry are still viewed as mortal enemies. When confronted with ideas that contradict their religious faith, otherwise bright and inquisitive students often fall back on childlike dogma and prepossession.

The problem would not be severe if it only occurred in philosophy or religion classes, but many other courses are likewise affected. Indeed when one examines the curriculum of modern liberal education, nearly everything written since the 12th or 13th century at least on first examination contradicts some commonly accepted Christian belief. In the natural sciences, astronomy from Copernicus to Einstein, Darwinian biology, and modern physicists' theories concerning the conservation of matter and energy are all counter to the literal interpretation of Scripture. In the social sciences, all liberally educated students encounter Freud's account of religious belief, Durkheim on the social forces behind religious experience, and Weber's work on capitalism and the Protestant ethic. In philosophy, Voltaire, Diderot, Spinoza, Rousseau, Hume, Marx, Nietzsche, Russell, Sartre, and even Kierkegaard are all either atheists or extremely critical of established Christian dogma and the organized church. Also, one can hardly take a course in European or American history without being exposed to such "high points" in church history as Galileo's plight, the Inquisition, or the Salem Witch Trials. The very scope of the antagonism between faith and critical inquiry creates significant problems for any professor who teaches liberal arts to classes comprised of medieval minds.

These theories, theorists, and incidents are central to the core of liberal education and cannot be dismissed with the typical "born again Christian" response that they are either the work of the devil or the authors simply "hadn't met Jesus." (Ironically, the critics of Christianity listed above are far better informed on theology and more familiar with the Bible than most current students who have "seen the light.") But if teaching in the liberal tradition must engage students in critical thought about their values and beliefs, how can one go about awakening students from their "dogmatic slumbers"? If students are a priori opposed to anything that contradicts their faith, how can liberal learning take place in those very institutions which define themselves as bastions of liberal education? This is an extremely important question for teachers in the church-related college. Students in these schools must be convinced there is nothing wrong with employing the gift of human reason to think critically about their faith.

SOLUTIONS

Church-related colleges are now faced with the dilemma of whether to emphasize liberal learning and critical thought or to support the dogmas of established religion. The graduate training of most professors in these institutions inclines them toward the former. Given the number of areas in many different subjects which either criticize or contradict commonly held Christian beliefs, ignoring these areas is tantamount to surrendering all claims to educating students liberally. My suggestion is that rather than prostituting liberal education to compliment our students' understanding (or misunderstanding) of religious faith, instructors in church-related colleges must turn students' emotional responses to criticisms of Christianity into opportunities for critical investigation. What initially appears as an obstacle to liberal learning becomes a blessing. Where historically liberal learning was understood as a process leading to Christian faith, today Christian faith may in fact be a means to liberal learning.

This opportunity for liberal learning may be unique to small church-related liberal arts colleges. Having taught at a large university for a few years (where the percentage of students committed to the unquestioning acceptance of Christian beliefs is smaller), I found that students tended to be interested neither in defending nor in critiquing Christian beliefs. At the state university not only is religion of less importance, but so also are the ideas of those thinkers in Western philosophy who are critical of Christianity. In a church-related institution, however, students' emotional interest in religion makes them naturally responsive—sometimes to the point of overt antagonism—to issues that have a bearing on their faith. Yet issues that challenge faith must be approached carefully, so that student attitudes toward critical thinking can be cultivated in a positive fashion.

What is the proper approach? It has been my experience that prior to any mention of religious issues in particular, students must become convinced of the value of free inquiry and critical analysis in general. Just as children must be taught that while going to the dentist may be painful, in the end they will be better off, so students must be taught that examining and defending their beliefs is ultimately in their own best interest. Conversely, students must be convinced that ignoring subjects or issues which challenge beliefs is harmful to them—just as the Church's attempts to squelch free inquiry in the Middle Ages ultimately harmed it. (Would the Reformation have occurred had the Catholic church welcomed dissent?)

For two reasons, I have found assigning John Stuart Mill's *On Liberty* (1956) especially useful in establishing the proper attitude toward critical thinking. First, Mill persuasively argues that to hold a belief without being willing to expose it to harsh criticism is to jeopardize the belief (because the belief which cannot stand up to intensive skeptical questioning is easily lost by the believer). As I suggested earlier, this is precisely the reason the Church initially saw liberal education as a valuable tool in spreading the faith. Ministers trained in the dialectic arts of criticism and persuasion could quite effectively dislodge the beliefs of the heretics or pagans, hence winning converts to Christianity. Also, the ministers themselves would not as easily lose beliefs which had been tested in the crucibles of dialectical inquiry. The point is analogous to Socrates' distinction between opinion and knowledge in the *Meno* (in Plato, 1956). Socrates points out that like the statues of Daedalus, one's opinions must be tied down; otherwise, they fly away—

For true opinions, as long as they stay, are splendid . . . , but they will not stay long—off and away they run out of the soul of mankind, so they are not worth much until you fasten them up with reasoning of cause and effect. (in Plato, 1956:65)

Religious faiths based on unexamined beliefs also easily "fly away," especially when confronted with the works of such thinkers as Freud, Marx, and Durkheim. Students who have a natural aversion to anything that contradicts their religious beliefs nevertheless can be persuaded that the examination and defense of faith is healthy for spiritual well-being and development. As Mill (1956:26) points out, even "the most intolerant of churches" recognize the value of a "devil's advocate." Given this perspective, studying such anti-Christian works as Nietzsche's *Thus Spoke Zarathustra* (1969) perhaps does students a spiritual favor.

Second, Mill also prescribes the reading of material which illustrates that the modern church and its members often lack the energy, commitment, and vitality of the early church fathers. Compared to the early Christians who risked their lives daily, modern believers tend to be passionless, uncommitted, spiritual anemics. Mill and Kierkegaard explain the modern

Christian lifelessness in terms of the dogmatic certainty believers have concerning their faith in a "Christian nation" where virtually everyone is a Christian. When all controversy over the truth of a creed ceases, the living power of the doctrine to inspire passionate enthusiasm declines. There remains, as Mill (1963:49) claims, only a "dull and torpid assent... until [the church] almost ceases to connect itself at all with the inner life of the human being." My experience is that most students—young and full of spiritual zest—are drawn to the enthusiasm of the early Christians and would like to change the modern religious torpor.

Once the importance of examining one's belief has been established, there are at least two other approaches that aid students in developing a willingness to engage in the critical study of material which contradicts their faith. One method which can be used in any class examining the Bible is to send students to the library to read scholarly commentaries on whatever passages are being studied. Students will quickly discover that biblical interpretations vary a great deal, and that it is naive to believe there is one and only one way to interpret Scripture. If the scholars disagree, why should freshmen in college believe they have the last word in biblical insight? Along these same lines, a study of the history and development of the Bible is useful. Most students see the Bible as something handed down by God and hence do not know that there have been great debates throughout history over which books should be included. The choice of chapters was usually made by virtue of consensus among groups of men and not by Divine decree. This knowledge is important because it brings into question the reasonableness of adopting a dogmatic attitude toward the absolute authority of Scripture.

Finally, I believe that students in a church-related liberal arts college need to be exposed to 20th-century liberal Christian theology. While it may be healthy for students to grapple with someone like Nietzsche, who so forcefully challenges the purity of Christian virtues, students may fail to take Nietzsche seriously because of his atheism. On the other hand, when well-known Christian thinkers—such as Reinhold Niebuhr and Paul Tillich—criticize Christian dogmatism and morality, the faithful tend to listen more intensely. For example, it is one thing for Nietzsche (1969) to accuse Christians of turning their backs on this world; it is quite another for students to read Niebuhr (1932) making the same criticism in light of the church's failure to deal with existing social problems. If academics such as Niebuhr can be critical of Christian otherworldly tendencies, students come to understand that there is really nothing wrong with criticism.

Tillich (1957) goes one step further by arguing that blind faith itself is heresy! Tillich claims that faith that is not critical of Christian dogma is in fact idolatry. Blind faith makes the earthly church and its articles of faith—and not God—an "ultimate concern." Healthy faith, on the other hand, requires uncertainty, doubt, and questioning. One must always remember that the church and all its truths are the products of finite human beings and are hence subject to error. According to Tillich (1948:226), true faith requires that:

there cannot be a sacred system, ecclesiastical or political; that there cannot be a sacred hierarchy with absolute authority; and there cannot be a truth in human minds which is divine truth in itself. Consequently, the prophetic spirit must always criticize, attack, and condemn sacred authorities, doctrines, and morals. . . . Each [person] has to decide for himself whether a doctrine is true or not.

While at first disconcerting to young students—who desire above all else for the truth to be simple and then simply to know the truth—eventually this attitude goes a long way toward demonstrating the value of liberal education. For if we each must decide for ourselves the truth of spiritual matters, what is needed above all else are the critical tools necessary for mature analysis and decision making. The acquisition of these tools is the culminating goal of liberal education. From this perspective, the liberal arts can be viewed as one of the greatest "friends of the faithful."

PROBLEMS

As suggested earlier, my recommendations are not without problems. After realizing the merit of critically evaluating beliefs, students often tell me they have lost their faith. I am never sure how to respond to these students. As a professional who has been hired to teach persons to be critical and reflective, I am not sure loss of faith should bother me. If students did not seriously question their beliefs in my courses, I would be failing to do my job. And if "losing one's faith" means the student has lost his or her naive, unreflective religious beliefs, it may be for the best from the point of view of spirituality. Real life is far more threatening and perilous than reading Nietzsche's *Thus Spoke Zarathustra*. The faith lost through reading some philosopher surely will not stand up to the tests of living. More importantly, the same critical tools which destroy a student's naive faith can also be employed to arrive at a more reasonable and defensible system of belief. The products of reason's crucible are far more durable than those one acquires without reflection and choice.

However, if the student follows in the Tillichean tradition of always searching, always questioning, always unwilling to accept any doctrine as "the truth," the question of *what* one has faith in becomes a problem. A person who claims faith in God must be able to define, at least in some elementary sense, the nature of God. Otherwise, belief is empty. For someone to say, "I believe in God, but I have no idea what God is like" is to render the word "God" unintelligible. While Tillich's approach to faith may be helpful in developing the critical spirit in the naive, unreflective believer, the consequences may be to strip the word "God" of all cognitive meaning. I can only suggest that perhaps, in the spirit of critical inquiry, students should be encouraged to find some half-way house between dogmatic and Tillichean theology. Perhaps it is time for instructors in church-related liberal arts colleges to encourage students to construct their own theologies which are consistent with their other beliefs and can withstand critical investigations. Perhaps students should be encouraged to see how many of their beliefs can be supported by reason and how many must be accepted on faith alone.

The problem with this approach may not be the responses of students but the complaints of parents and ministers who believe they have sent their children to a "nice Christian college" where the child's previous beliefs will be reinforced. Given that students probably acquired their attitudes toward religion from their parents and local ministers, perhaps it is time to invite these other parties to engage in a little "continuing education." Or perhaps it is time for church-related colleges to explain their mission as liberal arts institutions more clearly in their catalogues. Perhaps church-related colleges should go so far as to tell constituents that their immediate purpose is to give students a liberal education. The college catalogue might also state that although it is believed that such an education will ultimately enhance students' faith, such enhancement is not the real goal of liberal education. The goal of liberal education is to create mature, sensitive, and thoughtful citizens who can adequately analyze life's complex problems and arrive at reasonable and humane decisions. The means to this goal is to teach students to think clearly and critically about life's important issues—including religious faith.

12

Finding History in Your Backyard: The Merits of the Local History Seminar

GREGORY J. W. URWIN

SMALLNESS AND ISOLATION: BARRIERS TO HISTORICAL RESEARCH

Teaching in a small, four-year college presents many unique challenges for a professional historian. While I was earning my Ph.D. at the University of Notre Dame, I dreamed of finding work at a similar institution. Like most professional historians, I was trained to function in a research university. I envisioned myself as part of a large history department where I would concentrate primarily on studying and teaching United States military history.

However, as fate and a constricted academic job market would have it, my first full-time teaching appointment was at Saint Mary of the Plains College, a Catholic liberal arts institution located in Dodge City, the diminutive, dust-blown metropolis of rural southwest Kansas. Instead of joining a large history department, I became part of a trio. To complicate matters further, I was the only Americanist in the department. Rather than devoting my days to researching and lecturing about military affairs, I was now responsible for an entire American history curriculum. Thanks to my graduate training, I possessed a broad grounding in United States history, and I was reasonably equipped to meet my responsibilities. I cannot pretend that being a one-man American history department is easy. There are still numerous gaps in my education, and it will take years to fill them. Nevertheless, I believe I've been fairly successful at exposing my students to the salient facts and scholarly literature pertaining to this nation's history.

Yet lecturing about history and historiography is but a portion of a college history teacher's job. Just as important is the propagation of the teacher's profession, the molding of other historians. It is not enough to fill student's minds with facts or have them read great historical works. As Thomas E. Felt, senior historian of the New York State Education Department, observed, "Reading histories is an essential part of the historian's education, but only a part. Mere reading . . . yields only a fragment of the enjoyment to be found in trying to comprehend something about the past" (1976:xi). Students can become historians only by practicing a historian's skills. To put it plainly, budding historians must be permitted to *do* history— to research, to analyze, and to communicate their conclusions about the past in writing (Brownsword, 1973). I confess that when I first came to Saint Mary of the Plains College, I despaired of ever being able to school my students in the ways and wiles of the professional historian. The obstacles that stood in my path seemed insurmountable.

Saint Mary of the Plains is a relatively new college, founded in 1952. Like other institutions of its kind, it could do with a few more students and a larger operating budget. Because of the school's youth and financial constraints, its library holdings are relatively modest. Although the library possesses a respectable cross-section of the outstanding secondary works produced by historians over the past thirty years, it contains relatively few printed primary sources. Without a strong collection of contemporary records and eyewitness accounts in the school library, serious historical research appeared impossible.

This deficiency would not be a serious problem were Saint Mary of the Plains located near a large metropolitan area, an advantage enjoyed by some small colleges elsewhere in the United States. Were that the case, our students could avail themselves of the larger library collections of other colleges and universities. But Saint Mary of the Plains stands upon the spacious High Plains of southwest Kansas, a region characterized by sprawling wheat farms and small towns. The nearest university library is 100 miles to the north. Considering the many demands placed on the average undergraduate's time and pocketbook, it would be unfair for my colleagues or me to expect students to hop into a car and drive four or five hours every time they had to carry out in-depth historical research.

LOCAL HISTORY: THE CONVENIENT EXPEDIENT

Notwithstanding these difficulties, it is imperative that history majors engage in serious research. Whether they intend to go on to graduate school, teach history in primary or secondary schools, or enter a field outside of education, our students need to know how historians practice their craft. Our students need to develop basic research skills and to interpret the past. Denied that practical experience, their education would be incomplete, and the history program at my college would not be viable. Therefore, to provide my students with the opportunity actually to do history, I decided to offer a continuous cycle of seminars focusing on local history. A student historian at Saint Mary of the Plains would be hard-pressed to find enough primary sources to write an informed seminar paper about the political reforms of Sir Robert Peel or the monetary policies of the Grover Cleveland Administration, but he or she can find an abundance of material relating to the history of southwest Kansas. Indeed, to borrow a thought from John A. Neuenschwander (1976:12), the director of the Oral History Project of Carthage College, "the number of potential local studies is virtually limitless."

While southwest Kansas may lack impressive centers of industry or population, it is a region rich in history. Coronado passed through in the 1540s, and nearly 300 years later it was intersected by the Santa Fe Trail. That arid country was once the hunting ground of the Comanche, the Kiowa, the Arapaho, and the Cheyenne. It later became the theater of operations for soldiers like Stephen Watts Kearny, Philip Henry Sheridan,

William Tecumseh Sherman, George Armstrong Custer, Nelson A. Miles, and Richard I. Dodge, who helped wrest the region from the Plains tribes. In the 1870s, southwest Kansas was linked to the rest of the nation by the Atchison, Topeka, and Santa Fe Railroad, and it soon became the object of the legendary Long Drive. From 1875 until 1885, Dodge City reigned as the queen of the Kansas cow towns—a wild, wide-open railroad settlement, where millions of longhorns boarded trains bound for Eastern slaughterhouses and legions of Texas cowboys lost their hard-earned wages to a shady assemblage of frontier gamblers, saloonkeepers and prostitutes. This colorful era has been immortalized by countless "horse operas," such as the 1939 film *Dodge City* and the long-running television series *Gunsmoke*. Thanks to pulp fiction and Hollywood, Dodge City is better known around the world than many of our major cities. In fact, many Americans know more about Wyatt Earp and Bat Masterson than about some U.S. presidents. With the passing of the Long Drive and the arrival of the agricultural frontier, southwest Kansas ceased to interest the outside world. But the region recaptured America's headlines in the 1930s, when it was engulfed by the Dust Bowl.

The people of southwest Kansas are proud of their celebrated past. Indeed, they depend on it for much of their livelihood. Between 150,000 and 250,000 travelers visit the area each year to view reconstructions of Dodge City's Front Street and Boot Hill Cemetery, the remains of old Dodge City, and the hideout of the Dalton gang in nearby Meade, Kansas. The tourist trade is vital to the local economy, and many small entrepreneurs have learned that the lure of the past is a gateway to profits. The citizens of southwest Kansas have grown adept at exploiting their history, but they have also done much to preserve it too.

Thanks to this powerful historical consciousness, Dodge City contains two outstanding institutions that have proven indispensable to Saint Mary of the Plains' history students—Boot Hill Museum and the Kansas Heritage Center. Boot Hill Museum is dedicated to depicting Dodge City as it was during the era of the Long Drive. In addition to maintaining the Front Street and Boot Hill re-creations, the museum also possesses an extensive collection of manuscripts and artifacts relating to the history of southwest Kansas in the 1870s and 1880s. The Kansas Heritage Center is an equally valuable research facility. A joint project of Dodge City's Board of Education and the Kansas State Historical Society, the center is a well-stocked library established to serve the needs of local history teachers. Besides an impressive collection of films, slide shows, tapes, and other instructional aids, the center houses over 9,000 books covering the history of Kansas and the American West, including a number of published diaries, memoirs, and government papers. The center also owns microfilm copies of 65 separate small-town Kansas newspapers, which span the years 1876 until 1982, as well as census records from 21 Kansas counties for the years 1870 through 1915.

Even if there were no such places as Boot Hill Museum or the Kansas Heritage Center, it would still be possible to research local history in southwest Kansas. A college does not have to be situated in a town with a past as flamboyant as Dodge City's to support a meaningful local history program. Every county in America has its own courthouse, and I train my students to view each courthouse as a historical archive. Here an aspiring scholar may uncover a plentitude of primary sources—police reports, trial proceedings, voting statistics, birth and death records, marriage records, early militia rolls, local ordinances, property records, and other types of data—all of it the raw stuff of history. Furthermore, there is a wide variety of additional places where an ambitious young scholar may gather historical information—the annual economic reports stored at local chambers of commerce, the manuscript collections of local historical societies, the records assembled by local churches, boards of education, labor unions, and fire departments, the clippings files at the offices of local newspapers, the agricultural data available from county extension offices, the papers kept by local lawyers, contractors, and other businessmen, and the diaries, scrapbooks, and letters in the possession of private citizens (Penna, 1975; Felt, 1976). An enterprising student can unearth the traces of history almost anywhere. The list of historical repositories within easy reach is limited only by a student's imagination. Wherever men and women settled in this country, they left some written record of their experiences. Thus historians are able to reconstruct their lives and times. History lies wherever we care to look. It is important that we give our students the eyes to see it (Eckert, 1979).

One may exhume the past in other forms besides the written word. One of the local historian's most potent tools is oral history—the living testimony of those individuals who witnessed or participated in the events that shaped our own lives. As Weitzman (1979:16) claims:

Our own history is to be found in the memories of those closest to us, with whom we've grown up. The voices of our history speak, not in the practiced language of the historian, but in the vernacular of the settler and the accents of the immigrant.

Oral history can supplement written records or serve as reliable primary sources for incidents where no written documentation exists (Allen and Montell, 1981). As Allen and Montell (1981:56) have specifically argued: "oral accounts provide a wealth of detailed information that puts flesh on the bare bones of records and brings the events to life."

Through oral history, my students have met the founding fathers and mothers of many communities in southwest Kansas. These are the people who built the area's farms, businesses, churches, and schools; who saw depressions, droughts, and dust storms; who endured countless trials and held onto the land; who made southwest Kansas what it is today. Some of these people are just as colorful as the more notable figures one might meet in a textbook. My students have interviewed former bootleggers and Klansmen, a socialist politician who ran for governor in the 1930s, old soldiers, alumni of New Deal programs such as the Civilian Conservation Corps (CCC) or the Works Progress Administration (WPA), and maiden school marms who taught in one-room schoolhouses. Such people live in almost every community in America, and nothing pleases them more than talking about their lives (see Weitzman, 1979).

Thus by researching topics in local history, students at small colleges can receive a competent introduction to the historian's craft. They can work with the same types of materials that professional scholars use—official records, other sorts of manuscript sources, interviews, and printed primary sources. They can learn to appreciate if not completely master the rules of evidence, to understand the kind of digging and analysis that goes into writing sound history, which will help them to be more discriminating in their reading. If a research scholar teaches a student no more than what is listed above, it is a worthwhile undertaking. Yet the study of local history can teach students so much more.

THE HIDDEN BENEFITS OF A LOCAL HISTORY PROGRAM

When I first instituted my local history seminars, I regarded them as simple expedients—as a way to teach historical methodology in the absence of ample library resources. This is a prejudice shared by many professional historians (Allen and Montell, 1981). Since I began guiding my students through the study of local history, my outlook has changed. I no longer see the seminars as narrow academic exercises. These forays into local history have not only contributed to the development of my students, but they have also produced unexpected benefits for Saint Mary of the Plains and the community the college serves. What began in my mind as a necessary evil has been transformed into a positive good.

Years ago, local history was considered the province of amateurs and eccentrics, a not quite respectable enterprise just a few steps removed from genealogy (Sonnichsen, 1981). "Real" historians concerned themselves with the history of presidential administrations, national political systems, foreign affairs, and the great political, economic, and intellectual movements of the past. Happily, that flawed, elitist view has been corrected by the recent emergence of social history as one of the strongest branches of the historical profession. Perhaps the most refreshing characteristic of the new social history is its democratic thrust. Social historians have shown us that the essence of America is not to be found solely in the lives of its famous men and women or in the workings of a few national institutions. The American experience is a composite of the experiences of all Americans, no matter how lowly, and such ordinary folk can best be studied on the local level in small, easily defined groups. Local histories also reveal how national events, trends, personalities and institutions affected the general populace (Neuenschwander, 1976; Allen and Montell, 1981).

As a result of these developments, local history is no longer a frowned-upon hobby. Studies of ethnic minorities, urban neighborhoods, small towns, and rural counties are now hailed as effective tools for probing the American experience. Local history has been enthroned as the most convenient approach to the study of social history. This new orientation can give students a sense of standing on the cutting edge of the historical profession, of going places where scholars have never gone before. Participants in my local history seminars feel as if they are doing something more significant than earning a grade. They go about their work with a sense of adventure and purpose, attitudes a teacher should encourage.

One of my primary goals in the local history seminar is to demonstrate to students that they are performing a valuable service for their community by rescuing its past. Aside from the wild, cattle-town days of Dodge City and a few scattered references in general histories to the Santa Fe Trail, the Indian wars, and the Dust Bowl, southwest Kansas has largely escaped the attention of professional historians. As the only four-year institution of higher learning in southwest Kansas, Saint Mary of the Plains has an obligation to preserve and interpret the region's past. The message that I preach to my students, the local media, and local civic groups is simply this: "The time has come to give southwest Kansas its voice." Other small colleges serve regions suffering from the same inadequate historical coverage, and they could meet a real need by mobilizing their history faculties and students to reverse the situation. This mission would appeal strongly to the provincial loyalties of a rural community and to students whose families have deep roots in a given area.

Of course, no one expects an undergraduate to produce a ground-breaking scholarly treatise, but in their own way, I believe my seminar students are making solid contributions to the study of history. Through oral history, they are recording the reminiscences of numerous "old timers," testimony that might otherwise be lost forever. So much of our past lies buried and forgotten because no one took the trouble to preserve it. As the old saying goes, "history repeats itself because no one was listening the first time" (Szasz, 1975:213). Members of the generations that lived through the Great Depression or World War II are now in their fifties or older, and their ranks thin with each passing year. Their memories of these epochal crises are part of our heritage and should be saved. Some professors may consider the task of salvaging history as beneath their dignity, but the historical profession cannot afford such haughtiness. Dedicated as they may be, there are not enough archivists and librarians to save more than the highlights of America's past. They need assistance, and historians are their most natural allies (Sonnichsen, 1981). Should anyone require further persuasion, consider for a moment the African proverb: "When an old person dies, a library burns to the ground" (Allen and Montell, 1981:xii).

Local history seminars can aid in this valuable work by creating a corps of novice historians capable of preserving the testimony of elderly citizens. Saint Mary of the Plains College is supplying the workers necessary for preserving the history of southwest Kansas. Other small colleges can do the same for their localities. Hopefully, once the bug of doing history bites them, students will continue to study and preserve the past long after graduation.

To facilitate this work better, I have organized an informal network of middle-aged and senior citizens who are willing to talk to my students about whatever bits of local history they have experienced. With the assistance of the Saint Mary of the Plains' public relations office and the local media, this "Living Library of Southwest Kansas" sprang to life in the fall of 1983 with nearly 50 members, and its numbers have grown steadily ever since. When my students complete their seminar papers, they are encouraged to donate their interview tapes and notes, plus whatever additional primary documents they may have collected (such as photocopies of contemporary letters and diaries), to the college library. In time, Saint Mary of the Plains will house a respectable historical archive, which may be exploited by graduate students and professional scholars. Visits from other historians would have a stimulating effect on the college's history faculty and majors.

My students' activities as local historians have elicited favorable publicity and other encouraging responses from the surrounding community. The students have reflected a great deal of credit on themselves and on their college. Such community goodwill is a priceless asset for a small college, particularly one that is struggling to increase its endowment and enrollment.

Oral history is especially effective in closing the so-called generation gap. Most of our oral history subjects are flattered when they are contacted for interviews. They are also grateful to Saint Mary of the Plains for adding their stories to the area's collective memory. Each interview session is usually a revelation for both the interviewer and the interviewee. My students have gained an increased respect for their elders and the land in which they live. Oral history teaches budding scholars how to listen, an endangered art in this age of electronic media (Neuenschwander, 1976). For their part, the old timers come to see college students as serious, hard-working young adults with a real interest in the local area (see Neuenschwander, 1976; Weitzman, 1979).

At a time when most history departments complain of declining class enrollments, local history seminars may rekindle student interest in the past (Neuenschwander, 1976). The majority of those who participate in my seminars are not history majors. What attracts them to a class noted for its rigor? Allen and Montell (1981:7) answer this question when they claim that "local history deals with people and events we know best." It is often easier to excite students about the history of their own families or towns, rather than the Treaty of Ghent or the Walker Tariff. Furthermore, exposure to local history can infuse young people with a sense of identity and renewed pride in their origins. This is important, for even some of Saint Mary of the Plains' brightest students suffer from an inferiority complex—part of the price of growing up in small-town America. Weitzman (1979:16) has dubbed this positive consciousness as "the gift of history," which he describes in these words:

History is really getting back in touch.... In remembering and re-telling our ancestors' experiences we are actually going back to where we came from. Our reward is not so much a sense of "history" (what-ever that is) as a sense of who we are.

Local history seminars also train students to think critically about their surroundings, a habit which makes them better citizens. Finally, some of the people who enroll in local history classes are not full-time college students but adults—amateur historians and high school teachers wishing to expand their knowledge and polish their scholarly skills. A professor who promotes the study of local history is sure to win the approval of his or her college registrar.

In an age when the level of student literacy has taken an alarming plunge, the local history seminar offers historians the opportunity to help reverse this lamentable trend. Most professional historians are also professional writers—that is, they write for publication. They can impart knowledge of the writer's art which students would not ordinarily receive in the standard English composition course. I instruct my seminar students to write their papers as if they were preparing articles for academic journals, and I encourage the more successful to submit their work for publication and scholarly competitions. The thought that their papers may someday reach an audience operates as a powerful incentive on ambitious students. They become more willing to invest the time necessary to produce passable prose. By teaching students to raise their sights, it is possible to motivate them to raise their standards.

My experiences have convinced me of the merits of including a local history seminar in any undergraduate program. What began as a simple expedient has blossomed into a rewarding learning experience for both my students and me. At Saint Mary of the Plains College, more young people are being in-troduced to the arduous joys of doing history. My students are helping to preserve shreds of our precious heritage. They are learning to care more about other people, both living and dead. They are putting their time to good use by serving the local community. No professor could hope for more from any course.

13

Fishing in a Little Pond: Some Notes on Great Ideas in Small Colleges

JEFF GUNDY

A BEGINNING

One Saturday night in the spring of 1980 I was sitting at home when the phone rang. In my usual semi-alert Saturday night condition I answered, and the voice gave a name and said he was an associate dean at Hesston College in Kansas and had heard I might be interested in a job. I said huh, or something similar, and then as I woke up, I started to try to pronounce my final consonants and finish my sentences. Before long I was trying to explain my theory of teaching composition over the phone.

I hadn't really been looking for a job; I'd just started my dissertation and figured on one more year of hanging around Indiana University to finish it and nerve myself up to hit the job market. But the associate dean at Hesston knew the department chair at Goshen, where I'd interviewed but they'd hired somebody else ... anyway, the idea of making real wages instead of a teaching assistant's pittance didn't sound too bad. We flew out for an interview (they insisting my wife come too) and spent a whirlwind day talking to everybody who was anybody, and some who weren't, on campus.

Everyone seemed to want to warn us about the privations of life at a little church college on the blank plains of Kansas, and everyone was careful to call it "two-year" rather than "junior." Intellectual stimulation seemed to be the key phrase; everybody wanted at the same time to warn me not to expect too much, to justify their own being there despite that, and to let me in on the nuggets of satisfaction they had found. And there were signs that people were still alive, even thriving, in Kansas. At three-thirty I was talking to the dean when his secretary came in to remind him his recorder group was practicing. The guy who drove us back to the airport, a head resident in one of the dorms, was leaving to hitchhike across the country and then take a train across Russia, or some such wild scheme. We left feeling underwhelmed by the physical plant and the surroundings, even though Kansas is at its best in May; the trees looked harassed if not defeated, and the library where I was to have my office would fit comfortably in the lobby of Indiana University's. But we spent most of the flight back talking about how comfortable we'd felt with the people.

Two days after we got back they called and offered me a job, and my wife her choice of three: good secretaries were hard to come by in Kansas that year. In the middle of July we drove out to stay, through the 110° heat, bucking the headwinds in our old VW van. I kept a canteen beside me, to drink and pour over my shirt. When we finally got to Hesston, something made me go down to the college, damp and grungy as I was. When I walked into the dean's office he smiled, shook my hand, and agreed that the heat was incredible. Every building in town seemed to be air conditioned, though; the pool did terrific business, and people coped. It only rained twice in the next six months, but when it did, the water ran into our basement as though it had found the Promised Land. It felt like home.

ON FISHING IN SMALL PONDS

My college is owned by the Mennonite church, a denomination descended from Anabaptists who split from the Catholic church in Germany and the Netherlands during the Reformation. Mennonites have traditionally emphasized a simple life-style, nonresistance and pacifism, and a desire not always realized, to model their church on the active and communitarian church of the first centuries. Hesston has about 500 students these days, down from close to 700 in the glory days of the late 1970s. About half plan to go on to four-year schools, and the other half are in career programs—nursing, electronics, auto services, agriculture, and so on. Most are from rural or small-town backgrounds, most are middle-class, most are Mennonite by tradition if not by choice.

The general rule on campus is "Greet everything that moves." When I go back to Indiana or to the state university forty miles away, I feel half liberated and half oppressed by the people who pass me with no interest in saying hello. With the nearest real city 45 minutes away, the on-campus social life had better be good, and student services pours huge amounts of effort into keeping the students occupied: movies, square dances, roller skating, all kinds of dorm activities. By the time they graduate most of the students seem to know each other, and those of us who teach general education courses know at least half of them in one way or another.

By and large they are good students, though not fanatical ones, and much more interested in learning what they think will keep them comfortable later than in any abstract pursuit of truth. Many of the best students, especially in programs like English, come because their parents or brothers or girlfriends came here; few people with even moderate ambitions see one-person departments as the ideal place to learn their field. So I teach composition, lots of composition, with a literature course or creative writing class thrown in each semester for ten or twelve diehards, malcontents, and a few marginal types who think "short story" sounds easy because of the word "short."

One of the more innovative aspects of the Hesston curriculum is what we call the Foundation Studies Program, a general education program composed of four related courses that all students take, one per semester, during their two years with us. All four courses are interdisciplinary to some extent and seek to relate academic disciplines and processes to the issues and problems students must confront and the historic concerns of the Mennonite church: nonresistance, community of worship and interpretation, the effects of technology on life-style, the tension between faith as assent to propositions and faith as action in the world.

My most extensive involvement has been with the fourth of those courses, which aims to be a kind of capstone to the Hesston educational experience. We examine "concepts" like freedom, authority, order, rebellion, and conscience, and assign readings from all over the place, including some novels by people like Conrad, Dostoevsky, Camus, and Graham Greene. The novels, and the other materials as well, are chosen and discussed less for purely literary concerns (if there are such things) than for the ideas, issues and problems they present. I usually give a talk about looking for themes, one about characters, maybe one about symbols, and get a chance to read some poems and rave a little about life.*

The aim of the course is to give students at least some sense of the connections, so essential but so hard to see, between their lives and the choices they make and all the rest of the world; between their faith and their feelings and their functioning. We work at critical thinking, at separating thought from feeling, at connecting thought and action. We make a conscious effort to draw together various disciplines, genres, and media, and to convince students who may or may not ever take another college course that the habit of critical and reflective thinking is worth taking with them.

Recently I taught a small section of that course by myself for the first time—just 22 students, not the usual 150, but I did all the lecturing and all the discussion leading and all the grading. I had looked forward all fall with mingled fear and anticipation to the prospect of getting through five credit hours worth of material in three and a half weeks, running lengthy morning and afternoon sessions and still finding time to grade papers and plan lectures. I consoled myself somewhat with the thought of those talks on themes and symbols and character I had already worked up, but an odd thing happened when the

---

*The structure and content of this course were originally devised by Jim Mininger, academic dean at Hesston College. Much credit for any success I had with the course must go to him.

course actually got under way. I was just as busy as I'd feared, but despite that I found that when the whole course was mine, rather than just a few pieces of it, those talks on character and symbolism seemed considerably less crucial. I did read poems one afternoon, and we often talked briefly about literary concerns as part of our discussions, but I did substantially less lecturing on the formal aspects of reading literature than when that was my small part of a larger course.

Instead, we talked about literature, and art, and film, and history, and even a little science, but mostly we talked about the ideas that all those pieces and forms and means of inquiry suggested, evoked, and incarnated. We began by reading *1984*; we ended with Bonhoeffer's *Cost of Discipleship*, and along the way we examined Robert Bly's anti-Vietnam poems, Jacob Bronowski's exploration of the Uncertainty Principle and its relevance to human ethics, Dostoevsky's "Grand Inquisitor" and *Notes from Underground*, *The Great Gatsby*, liberation theology, Gary Snyder's *The Old Ways*, *Dr. Strangelove*, and Robert MacNamara's ideas about reducing the risk of nuclear war. Among other things.

The students were mostly nursing students who couldn't get the course in during the regular semester; many of them were older, married, with families to tend, and the strain of cramming five credit hours worth of great ideas into three and a half weeks had us all frazzled by the end. Yet in many ways it was one of the best teaching experiences I've ever had, despite—or perhaps because—it forced me outside of my role as English teacher. Most of the students in the course were the kind that never show up in English classes unless they're forced to, but now they read and discussed and wrote about Orwell and Dostoevsky and Bly not only dutifully but with real engagement. The discussions were intense, sometimes passionate, and all through the term I kept running into little knots of students all over the campus, leaning against the walls and arguing about order or freedom or authority.

Why? All I know to suggest is that I made no attempt to make Literature, capital L, and the theoretical and technical terms that attach to it, anything more than a means to an end, which as I told them on the first day, was both very simple and

too large a task for anyone to complete: to come to see the
actual order of the universe we inhabit, to recognize that all
our actions affect that order, and to attempt to learn how to
act responsibly. In order to know, we read and talked and wrote,
and talked about how best to read and to write, but the vocab-
ulary that emerged was weighted with moral and ethical terms,
not with technical ones.

Perhaps the most important aspect of the course, though we
seldom mention it to students, is its innately interdisciplinary
content and structure. In a fairly typical unit students read
essays by Martin Luther and Dietrich Bonhoeffer, a section of
Erich Fromm's *Escape from Freedom*, Orwell's *1984*, and "Six
Winter Privacy Poems" by Robert Bly, and see and discuss the
film *Shane*. What impressed me was how quickly the students
learned to deal with changing genres and styles, to see into
the essentials without ignoring the details. As we examined
each of these works, focusing on the theme of freedom, students
began very quickly to draw lines of connection and tension
between the theological prose of Luther and Bonhoeffer,
Fromm's analysis of the social forces behind Nazism, Orwell's
grim warning about totalitarianism, Bly's free-wheeling natural mysticism, and the frontier mythology of *Shane*. Not conditioned into academic schools that separate the best that has
been thought and said into artificial categories, they were ready
at least to begin to look at the world of thought as one, to begin
to see that nothing is irrelevant.

Many teachers here, and I think elsewhere, struggle constantly to bring the social and political ideals we formed in the
1960s into the relentlessly pragmatic 1980s. But my experience
suggests that no matter how practical the time, there are levels
of responsibility even the most ruthless recognize. The idealism
of the 1960s may be gone, but even the most self-centered
students are not beyond realizing that there is little future for
them on a radioactive cinder. If confronted with the realities
of Central America or South Africa, most are ready to recognize
their involvement and their responsibility. Students with a
religious tradition of pacifism and social action may be more
than usually ready to be educated on such matters, but one of
the most involved and energetic, if not credulous, students in

the course was a 50-year-old Methodist woman now back in school after raising her children. But she and the others kept coming back to the essential question, one I had no real answer for: What are we to do?

Most students come to college with a shallow cynicism or an optimism just as shallow, both of which serve to rationalize their ignoring anything too uncomfortable or personally threatening, and both of which are in our students usually closely related to their religious heritage, which tends to be strong but a touch simplistic. They need to be confronted with the paradoxes and tensions of the human condition, not to destroy their faith, but to make it one that can stand a full look at things. They need to be prodded toward action, but the problem of what and how is the most difficult of all. A few always manage to ask us what we, who talk so impressively to them, are doing ourselves, and then we squirm a little. Passing our time in the center of Kansas, that's what, complaining about our 12-year-old cars and our 80-year-old houses, raising our children and our gardens, not living the American Dream to the hilt but not exactly suffering either. Is it enough? Probably not. But it's what we can do, here, now.

THE TRUE NATURE OF THE UNIVERSE

When I started college at the very end of the 1960s, I somehow got the idea that I was in school to learn how to be the best person I could be, which meant first learning what I could about life and also learning what I could and should do about it. And always to have fun, of course. At a small church college in Indiana I managed all those things pretty well, as far as I could tell, but when I decided to take courses in things like history and philosophy instead of education, I found I had not left myself particularly employable. So I worked in a sash and door factory for a year, which was the kind of experience people say builds character, then escaped back into graduate school. During that first year I went back to my college town and was talking to an old friend, and I suddenly found myself saying, "You know, Troyer, some of those people don't even believe there is a true nature of the universe." He laughed, I laughed, and we went on talking. But that little phrase has been rattling around in my head ever since.

I didn't know what I meant by it then. I'm not sure I do now. But it has something to do with an attitude toward learning, toward experience, toward life. I was skeptical-verging-on-hostile about much of the instruction, especially religious instruction, I got as an undergraduate; I scoffed as loudly as anyone at all the highminded talk about piety and community and social involvement. But at the state university, suddenly surrounded by high-powered scholarship and people who actually wrote those textbooks that had always seemed to come direct from some academic version of Yahweh, I began to realize that scholarship in itself was a worthy pursuit but not the only one.

I didn't suddenly turn into a model of orthodoxy. Far from it. But I did come to value and seek out the frame of mind in which both ultimate questions and the links between ultimate issues and particular, immediate actions are kept constantly before me, not always in a solemn or even serious way, certainly not in a dogmatic way. I began to hope that some day I could work with others with that same desire, as well as teach composition and creative writing and modern poetry and all the rest.

I first got interested in literature as a discipline because it seemed the people teaching it were engaging most directly the things that seemed to matter: the fragility, beauty, and terror of the natural world, the grace and violence of the human spirit, the search for knowledge of the intricate web of the universe. As I went from college to graduate school to teaching, I found that pursuing those interests led me not only deeper into literature, but back out into other disciplines as well. I discovered that scholars in many fields were pursuing lines of inquiry that seemed to shed light on my study of modern American poetry and aid my efforts to teach. Modern biology, sociology, philosophy, psychology, political science, physics, and history all have helped me to see into our time and its literature; among other things that literature is a quite direct product of and response to the explosion of study taking place in all those fields and others. Conversely, the study of literature remains for me one of the most direct ways into the crucial questions of our time, and all time, because it works not through the distant categories of abstractions but through the vital immediacies of character, plot, and image.

It is not a simple thing to pursue the true nature of the universe from a small two-year college in Kansas, much less to convince students that such a pursuit has a place beside computer programming or accounting in their studies. We clearly need people who can run computers and businesses and work on cars. But we also need people who can and will reflect on their work and their lives in larger contexts, from the local community to the interconnection of all life on the planet. And so I cherish the times when I can forget about trying to convince freshman of the advantages of thesis sentences and talk with them about their lives and mine and the world we must, between all of us, somehow preserve. Surely good teachers find ways to do that everywhere, in all kinds of courses, at all kinds of schools. But it happens in the small ponds, too.

Bibliography

Adams, James A. 1984. "Networked computers promote computer literacy and computer-assisted instruction." *T.H.E. Journal* 11:95–99.

Allen, Barbara, and Lynwood Montell. 1981. *From memory to history: Using oral sources in local historical research*. Nashville, TN: American Association for State and Local History.

Aquinas, St. Thomas. 1982. *The summa theologica, five volumes*. Westminster, MD: Christian Classics.

Aristotle. 1941. *The basic works of Aristotle*. Ed. Richard McKeon. New York: Random House.

Association of American Colleges. 1982. "Teaching about values and ethics." *Forum for Liberal Education* 3:1–18.

———. 1985. *Integrity in the college curriculum: A report to the academic community*. Washington, DC: Author.

Astin, Alexander W. 1977. *Four critical years*. San Francisco: Jossey-Bass.

———. 1982. *Minorities in American higher education*. San Francisco: Jossey-Bass.

———. 1984a "Student involvement: A developmental theory for higher education." *Journal of College Student Personnel* 25:297–308.

———. 1984b "Student values: Knowing more about where we are today." *American Association for Higher Education Bulletin* 9:10–13.

Astin, Alexander W., and Calvin B. T. Lee. 1971. *The invisible colleges: A profile of small, private colleges with limited resources.* New York: The Carnegie Commission on Higher Education (Mc-Graw-Hill).

Astin, Alexander W., and Robert J. Panos. 1969. *The educational and vocational development of college students.* Washington, DC: American Council on Education.

Attewell, Paul, and James Rule. 1984. "Computing and computers: What we know and what we don't know." *Communications of the ACM* 12:1184–92.

Awalt, R. K., and Ben L. Gee. 1983 "Microprocessors in a network top mainframe in performance." *Electronics* 24:122–26.

Bailie, D. F., and E. T. Hall. 1975. "A small college cooperative seminar." *American Mathematical Monthly* 82:754–55.

Baker, Paul J., and Mary Zey-Ferrell. 1984. "Local and cosmopolitan orientations of faculty: Implications for teaching." *Teaching Sociology* 12:82–106.

Bales, Robert F., and Philip E., Slater. 1955. "Role differentiation in small decision-making groups." Pp. 259–306 in Talcott Parsons and Robert F. Bales (eds.), *Family, socialization, and interaction processes.* New York: Free Press.

Barker, Roger G., and Paul V. Gump. 1964. *Big school, small school.* Stanford, CA: Stanford University Press.

Bergquist, W. H., and S. R. Phillips. 1975. *A handbook for faculty development,* Volume 1. Washington, DC: Council for Advancement of Small Colleges.

———. 1977. *A handbook for faculty development,* Volume 2. Washington, DC: Council for Advancement of Small Colleges.

———. 1981. *A handbook for faculty development,* Volume 3. Washington, DC: Council for Advancement of Small Colleges.

Bess, James L. (ed.). 1982. *New directions for teaching and learning: Motivating professors to teach effectively.* San Francisco: Jossey-Bass.

Bloom, B. S., M. D. Englehart, E. J. Furst, W. H. Hill, and D. R. Krathwohl. 1956. *Taxonomy of educational objectives, handbook one: Cognitive domain.* New York: David McKay.

Bradley, R. J., and S. E. Williams. 1982. "Educating society for the information age." *Data Management* 11:28.

Brady, T. S. 1984. "Six step method to long range planning for non-profit organizations." *Managerial Planning* 32: 47–50.

Brand, Stewart (ed.). 1984. *The whole earth software catalog.* New York: Doubleday (Quantum).

Bray, David W. 1984. "Using personal computers at the college level." *IEEE Computer* 4:36–43.

Brownsword, Alan W. 1973. "Doing history: A skills approach." *The History Teacher* 6:251–66.

Buber, Martin. 1970. *I and thou.* New York: Scribner's.

Buckner, Janice, and Elliott Haugen. 1983. "Integrating microcomputers into the non-computer science curriculum: A team approach." *Proceedings of the 16th Annual Small College Computing Symposium.* Northfield, MN: Small College Computing Symposium.

Business Week. 1984. "Artificial intelligence is here." *Business Week* 2850 (July 9):54–62.

Chambers, John C., Satinder K. Mullick, and Donald D. Smith. 1971. "How to choose the right forecasting technique." *Harvard Business Review* 49 (July-August):45–74.

Chickering, Arthur W. (ed.). 1981. *The modern American college.* San Francisco: Jossey-Bass.

Cooley, Charles Horton. 1909. *Social organization.* New York: Scribner's.

Cubberley, Ellwood Patterson. 1920. *The history of education.* New York: Houghton Mifflin.

Dalrymple, Rick. 1984. "Software portability issues confront computer DEMS." *Mini-Micro Systems* 8:113.

Davis, Murray S., and Catherine J. Schmidt. 1977. "The obnoxious and the nice." *Sociometry* 40: 201–13.

Dight, Janet. 1984. "A guide to DP training." *Datamation* 29:202–4.

Dodrill, W. H. 1982. "Computer support for teaching large enrollment courses." *ACM SIGCSE* 1:31.

Dressel, Paul L., and Dora Marcus 1982. *On teaching and learning in college.* San Francisco: Jossey-Bass.

Eble, Kenneth E. 1972. *Professors as teachers.* San Francisco: Jossey-Bass.

———. 1976. *The craft of teaching.* San Francisco: Jossey-Bass.

———. 1983. *The aims of college teaching.* San Francisco: Jossey-Bass.

Eckert, Edward K. 1979. "Local history: Everyone's hidden treasure." *The History Teacher* 13:31–35.

Ellner, C. L. 1983. "Piercing the college veil." Pp. 183–93 in C. L. Ellner and C. P. Barnes (eds.), *Studies in college teaching: Experimental results, theoretical interpretations, and new perspectives.* Lexington, MA: D. C. Heath.

Ellner, C. L. and C. P. Barnes (eds.). 1983. *Studies in college teaching: Experimental results, theoretical interpretations, and new perspectives.* Lexington, MA: D. C. Heath.

Erikson, Kai T. 1976. *Everything in its path: Destruction of community in the Buffalo Creek flood.* New York: Simon and Schuster.

Feldman, Kenneth A. 1976. "The superior college teacher from the student's view." *Research in Higher Education* 5:243–88.

Felt, Thomas E. 1976. *Researching, writing and publishing local history.* Nashville, TN: American Association for State and Local History.

Flanders, Harley. 1971. "A survival kit for the college mathematician." *American Mathematical Monthly* 78:291–96.

Fox, M. F., and C. A. Faven. 1984. "Independence and cooperation in research: The motivations and costs of collaboration." *Journal of Higher Education* 55:347–59.

Friedrich, Robert J., and Stanley J. Michalak, Jr. 1983. "Why doesn't research improve teaching? Some answers from a small liberal arts college." *Journal of Higher Education* 54:145–63.

Froehlich, Robert A. 1984. *The free software catalog and directory.* New York: Crown.

Fuhrman, B. S., and A. F. Grasha. 1983. *A practical guide for college teachers.* Boston: Little, Brown.

Gaff, J. G. 1976. *Toward faculty renewal: Advances in faculty, instructional, and organizational development.* San Francisco: Jossey-Bass.

Gaff, S., C. Festa, and J. G. Gaff. 1978. *Professional development: A guide to resources.* New Rochelle, NY: Change Magazine Press.

Gibson, Cyrus F., and Richard L. Nolan. 1974. "Managing the four stages of EDP growth." *Harvard Business Review* 52 (January–February):76–88.

Goffman, Erving. 1961. *Encounters: Two studies in the sociology of interaction.* Indianapolis, IN: Bobbs-Merrill.

Goldsmid, Charles A., and Everett K. Wilson. 1980. *Passing on sociology: The teaching of a discipline.* Belmont, CA: Wadsworth.

Goode, William J. 1967. "The protection of the inept." *American Sociological Review* 32:5–19.

Gouldner, Alvin W. 1957. "Cosmopolitans and locals: Toward an analysis of latent social roles—part 1." *Administrative Science Quarterly* 2:281–306.

Gullette, Margaret Morganroth (ed.). 1982. *The art and craft of teaching.* Cambridge, MA: Harvard University Press.

Hall, Alfred E. 1984. "Starting at the beginning—the baccalaureate origins of doctorate recipients, 1920–1980." *Change* 16(3):40–43.

Hall, D. E., D. K. Sherrer, and J. S. Sventek. 1980. "A virtual operating system." *Communications of the ACM* 9:495–502.

Harrow, Keith. 1982. "A faculty development program." *ACM SIGCSE* 1:170–73.

Hastings Center Institute of Society, Ethics and the Life Sciences. 1980. *The teaching of ethics in higher education.* Hastings-on-Hudson, NY: Author.

Henschen, Keith. 1977. "Unpublished lecture at the University of Utah College of Health." (July 18). Salt Lake City, UT.

Hiltz, S. R. 1982. "Human diversity and the choice of interface: A design challenge." *ACM SIGCSE* 2:125–30.

Hindin, Harvey J. 1983. "Software strives toward portability with two steps in the right direction." *Electronics* 24:127.

Hirsch, Alan. 1983. "New spreadsheet packages do more than model." *Mini-Micro Systems* 7:205–12.

Hoffman, Paul W. 1985. "President's report to the board of trustees." Photocopied address. (March). McPherson, KS: McPherson College.

Hoffman, R. A. 1984. "An assessment of the teaching, research, and service function of a college faculty." *Journal of Research and Development in Education* 17:51–54.

Hofstadter, Douglas R. 1979. *Godel, Escher, Bach: An eternal golden braid.* New York: Basic Books.

Holtz, Herman. 1983. *How to succeed as an independent consultant.* New York: Wiley-Interscience.

Howe, Irving (ed.). 1983. *1984 revisited: Totalitarianism in our century.* New York: Harper & Row.

Hughes, Robert V. 1983. "Before you leap into the computer age with both feet, take these five deliberate steps." *The American School Board Journal* 170:28–29.

Irvine, C. A., and Mark Overgaard. 1983. "P-system network lets dissimilar computers share resources." *Electronics* 24:133–38.

Kasulis, Thomas P. 1982. "Questioning." Pp. 38–48 in Margaret Morganroth Gullette (ed.), *The art and craft of teaching.* Cambridge, MA: Harvard University Press.

Keen, Peter G. W., and Lynda A. Woodman. 1984. "What to do with all those micros." *Harvard Business Review* 62(5):142–50.

Kelley, S., Jr., R. E. Ayres, and W. G. Bowen. 1967. "Registration and voting: Putting first things first." *American Political Science Review* 67:359–79.

Kenealy, Patrick. 1983. "Product profile: Small business systems." *Mini-Micro Systems* 7:151–92.

Kerridge, J. M. 1982. "A simulator for teaching computer architecture." *ACM SIGCSE* 1:2.

Killian, Joyce E. 1985. "Fostering computer competence in schools." *Educational Leadership* 42:81–83.

Killmon, Peg. 1984. "Mass storage devices keep pace with system needs." *Computer Design* 11:71–81.

Komoski, P. Kenneth. 1983. "Use these five ideas when drafting computer policies." *The American School Board Journal* 170:30.

Krutch, Joseph W. 1929. *The modern temper: A study and a confession.* New York: Harcourt.

Langerak, Edward. 1982. "Values in the curriculum." *Forum for Liberal Education* 3:2–4.

Lerner, Eric J. 1984. "ICs nudging the submicron geometry limit." *Electronics Week* 35:51–58.

Levin, Dan. 1983. "Everybody wants "computer literacy," so maybe we should know what it means." *The American School Board Journal* 170:25–28.

Lindquist, J., W. H. Bergquist, C. Mathis, C. H. Case, T. Clark, and L. C. Buhl. 1979. *Designing teaching improvement programs.* Washington, DC: Council for Advancement of Small Colleges.

Linton, Ralph. 1936. *The study of man.* New York: Appleton-Century.

McCulloch, A. M. 1979. "Teaching: Who cares?" *Teaching Political Science* 6:493–507.

McFarlan, F. Warren, James L. McKenney, and Philip Pyburn. 1983. "The information archipelago—plotting a course." *Harvard Business Review* 61 (1):145–56.

McGee, Reece. 1971. *Academic Janus: The private college and its faculty.* San Francisco: Jossey-Bass.

McGregor, Scott, and Andrea Lewis. 1983. "Windowing software gives bit-mapped screen a graphics interface." *Electronics* 24:128–32.

McKeachie, Wilbert J. 1969. *Teaching tips: A guidebook for the beginning college teacher* (6th ed.). Lexington, MA: D. C. Heath.

———. 1978. *Teaching tips: A guidebook for the beginning college teacher* (7th ed.). Lexington, MA: D. C. Heath.

Mace, Myles L. 1975. "The president and corporate planning." In Harvard Business Review Editors (eds.), *Harvard Business Review—on Management.* New York: Harper and Row.

Mandell, Richard D. 1977. *The professor game.* New York: Doubleday.

Manuel, Tom, and Stephen Evanczuk. 1983. "Commercial products begin to emerge from decades of research." *Electronics* 24:127–31.

Martin, Warren B. 1982. *College of character.* San Francisco: Jossey-Bass.

Masland, Andrew T. 1984. "Cultural influences on academic computing: implications for liberal education." *Liberal Education* 70:83–90.

May, Rollo. 1975. *The courage to create.* New York: W. W. Norton.

Mayhew, Lewis B. 1979. *Surviving the eighties.* San Francisco: Jossey-Bass.

Medlin, William K. 1964. *The history of educational ideas in the West.* New York: Center for Applied Research in Education.

Merton, Robert K. 1957. *Social theory and social structure* (rev. ed.). New York: Free Press.

———. 1976. *Sociological ambivalence and other essays.* New York: Free Press.

Mikkelson, R. C., and Charles R. Green. 1983. "Faculty development and real-time computing." Pp. 141–60 in the *Proceedings of the 16th Annual Small College Computing Symposium.* Northfield, MN: Small College Computing Symposium.

Mill, John Stuart. 1956. *On liberty.* Indianapolis, IN: Bobbs-Merrill.

Minter, John W. 1985. Personal communication (June 11).

Morreale, Ben. 1972. *Down and out in academia.* Marshfield, MA: Pitman.

Morrill, Richard L. 1978. "A conceptual basis for values education in the university." *Soundings* 4:421–38.

———. 1982. "Values and the education of conscience: The role of the university." Pp. 42–71 in *The role of the university in the search for international values consensus.* New York: Rockefeller Foundation.

Moyer, Reed. 1984. "The futility of forecasting." *Long Range Planning* 1:65–72.

Naisbitt, John. 1982. *Megatrends: Ten new directions transforming our lives.* New York: Warner.

National Center for Educational Statistics. 1983–84 *Digest of Educational Statistics.* Washington, DC: U.S. Government Printing Office.

National Institute of Education. 1984. *Involvement in learning: Realizing the potential of American higher education.* Washington, DC: U.S. Department of Education.

Neuenschwander, John A. 1976. *Oral history as a teaching approach.* Washington, DC: National Educational Association.

Niebuhr, Reinhold. 1932. *Moral man and immoral society.* New York: Scribner's.

Nietzsche, Friedrich. 1969. *Thus spoke Zarathustra.* Translated by R. J. Hollingdale. New York: Penguin Classics.

O'Brien, Gael M. 1976. "Colleges' concern grows over ethical values." *Chronicle of Higher Education* 11(February 23):5.

Parsons, Talcott. 1951. *The social system.* New York: Free Press.

Penna, Anthony N. 1975. "Schools as archives." *The History Teacher* 9: 19–28.

Peters, T. J., and R. H. Waterman. 1982. *In search of excellence: Lessons from America's best-run companies.* New York: Harper & Row.

Pfeffer, Jeffrey. 1981. *Power in organizations*. Marshfield, MA: Pitman.

Plato. 1956. *Great dialogues of Plato*. Translated by W. H. Rouse. New York: New American Library.

Ratner, L. A. 1981. "Creating shared values through dialogue: The role of the chief academic officer." *New Directions for Teaching and Learning* 5:17–24.

Redfield, Robert. 1941. *The folk culture of Yucatan*. Chicago: University of Chicago Press.

————. 1947. "The folk society." *America Journal of Sociology* 52:293–308.

Resource Center on Sex Roles in Education. 1977. *Implementing Title IX and attaining sex equity in education*. Washington, DC: National Foundation for the Improvement of Education.

Rich, Harvey E., and Pamela M. Jolicoeur. 1978. "Faculty role perceptions and preferences." *Sociology of Work and Occupations* 5:432–45.

Riggs, Henry E. 1983. *Managing high-technology companies*. Belmont, CA: Wadsworth.

Rogers, Carl. 1983. *Freedom to learn for the 80s*. Columbus, OH: Charles E. Merrill.

Rosecrance, Francis C. 1962. *The American college and its teachers*. New York: Macmillan.

Rudolph, Frederick. 1962. *The American college and university: A history*. New York: Vintage.

Sacks, Howard, and Terry Weiner. 1978. *Some problems of teaching sociology in small departments and some tentative solutions*. Washington, DC: American Sociological Association Teaching Resources Center.

Seligman, Martin, and David Rosenhan. 1984. *Abnormal Psychology*. New York: W. W. Norton.

Shank, J. K., E. G. Niblock, and W. T. Sandalls, Jr. 1975. "Balance 'Creativity' and 'Practicality' in Formal Planning." In Harvard Business Review Editors (eds.), *Harvard Business Review—on Management*. New York: Harper & Row.

Simpson, David R. 1984. "Desktop plotters draw attention via price cuts and color capabilities." *Mini-Micro Systems* 8: 185–216.

Sloan, Douglas (ed.). 1980. *Education and values*. New York: Teacher's College Press (Columbia University).

Snavley, Guy E. 1955. *The church and the four year college*. New York:. Harper & Row.

Sonnichsen, C. L. 1981. *The ambidextrous historian: Historical writers and writing in the American West*. Norman, OK: University of Oklahoma Press.

Stieffel, Malcolm L. and David R. Simpson. 1983. "Minicomputer spreadsheets take advantage of hardware capabilities." *Mini-Micro Systems* 7:172–78.

Szasz, Ferenc M. 1975. "The many meanings of history, part 3." *The History Teacher* 8:208–17.

Tillich, Paul. 1948. *Dynamics of faith*. New York: Harper & Row.

———. 1957. *The Protestant era*. Chicago: University of Chicago Press.

Toennies, Ferdinand. 1957. *Gemeinschaft und Gesellschaft* (Community and society). East Lansing, MI: Michigan State University Press.

Trudeau, R. H., M. S. Hyde, and J. M. Carlson. 1982. "A data center for an undergraduate college." *News for Teachers of Political Science* 34:1–2.

Tucker, Norma. 1984. "Kansas college graduates are high achievers." *Kansas Independent Colleges* (Summer):3.

Weitzman, David. 1979. "The gift of history." *The American West* 16: 16–19, 62–63.

Wolcowitz, Jeffrey. 1982. "The first day of class." Pp. 10–24 in Margaret Morganroth Gullette (ed.), *The art and craft of teaching*. Cambridge, MA: Harvard University Press.

Wright, Richard A. 1976. "The dialectic of pronouns: A critical assessment of the folk-urban tradition in sociology." *Sociological Focus* 9:381–88.

———. 1984. "A structural theory of equilibrium, disequilibrium and change." *Free Inquiry in Creative Sociology* 12:. 144–50.

Name Index

Subject Index

University model, for higher education, 21, 23–24, 58,
105–6

Values education: and critical
values, 59–60; and curriculum, 58–64; and the discipline
of ethics, 66–68; and ethical
competence, 62; in the small
college, 57–58; and value

analysis, 68; and values criticism, 69; and values con-
sciousness, 68–69; and values
development, 64–66
Videotaping, of instruction, 41,
43–44, 50–51

"We" orientation, 29–31, 33–34,
36

About the Contributors

JOHN A. BURDEN has been teaching at McPherson College, McPherson, Kansas, for eleven of the past thirteen years. He received the B.A. (philosophy) and M.A. (psychology) degrees from Western Kentucky University. He has studied the psychology of organizations for two years at the University of Tennessee.

PAUL N. GRABER is an Associate Professor of Physical Education and Director of Athletics at McPherson College in McPherson, Kansas. He earned his Ph.D. degree in physical education administration from the University of Utah in 1979. His primary research interests are in physical education history and sports psychology. In addition to his teaching and administrative work, Dr. Graber has coached interscholastic and intercollegiate athletics for sixteen years.

JEFF GUNDY was born on a farm in central Illinois and attended Goshen College, where he published two chapbooks of poetry. His 1983 Ph.D. dissertation on the self in modern poetry was nominated for the Esther L. Kinsley Award, given annually to three outstanding dissertations at Indiana University. From 1980 to 1984 he taught literature, writing, and humanities and chaired the English Department at Hesston College in Hesston, Kansas. He has published numerous poems and reviews in magazines and journals, including *Kansas Quarterly*, *Mid-American Review*, *Indiana Review*, and *Cottonwood Review*. He is currently Associate Professor of English at Bluffton College in Bluffton, Ohio.

DONALD HATCHER is an Assistant Professor of Philosophy and Religion at Baker University in Baldwin City, Kansas. He is currently Director of Baker University's Science, Technology, and Human Values Program. He is the author of *Understanding "The Second Sex"* (Peter Lang Publishing, forthcoming) and "Creativity and the Socratic Notion of Education" (*The Journal of General Education*, forthcoming). He has also presented a number of papers at professional meetings on the subjects of technology and ethics, and the philosophy of religion.

JAMES K. McREYNOLDS completed his doctoral studies at United States International University. He has taught psychology for ten years in a one-person department at St. Mary of the Plains College in Dodge City, Kansas.

RICHARD S. REMPEL received his B.A. at Bethel College in North Newton, Kansas, M.A. from the University of Kansas, and Ph.D. from the University of Illinois at Champaign-Urbana, all in mathematics. He has taught at Bethel College since 1972, except for a sabbatical year at the Behavioral Sciences Institute in Boulder, Colorado. He recently finished a term as Chairman of the Cooperative Mathematical Sciences Department (described in his chapter).

DAVID CHARLES SMITH is Executive Director of the Society for Values in Higher Education, located at the Yale Divinity School in New Haven, Connecticut. The society is an association of faculty members in many disciplines, college and university administrators, and persons in the professions who are mutually concerned with the effective teaching of values. Dr. Smith's academic background is in the history of Christianity.

He currently directs a society-sponsored national project on Values and Decision-Making in Higher Education. Dr. Smith co-teaches a course on ministry and higher education at Yale Divinity School.

GREGORY J. W. URWIN received his Ph.D. from the University of Notre Dame. From 1982 until 1984, he taught American history at St. Mary of the Plains College in Dodge City, Kansas, where he instituted a prize-winning local history program. He is currently Assistant Professor of History at the University of Central Arkansas in Conway. Dr. Urwin is the author of two books—*Custer Victorious: The Civil War Battles of General George Armstrong Custer* (Fairleigh Dickinson University Press, 1983) and *The United States Cavalry: An Illustrated History* (Blandford Press, 1983)—and over 70 articles.

JAN P. VERMEER is Associate Professor of Political Science, Head of the Department of Political Science, and Chairman of the Division of Social Sciences at Nebraska Wesleyan University in Lincoln, Nebraska. His research interests encompass both campaigns and election, and the media and politics. He is the author of *"For Immediate Release": Candidate News Releases in American Political Campaigns* (Greenwood Press, 1982).

ROBERT L. WARD is the Coordinator of the popular C User's Group, an international organization whose membership includes over 3,100 practicing C programmers. He is an expert on the practical C utilities needed for program development. He is also a design consultant specializing in microprocessor-based communications equipment. Robert Ward is Assistant Professor of Computer Science at McPherson College in McPherson, Kansas.

RICHARD A. WRIGHT is Associate Professor of Sociology and Criminology at McPherson College in McPherson, Kansas. His primary research interests are in criminology, sociological theory, and teaching sociology. He has over 80 publications, including two other edited books—*Crime and Control: Syllabi and Instructional Materials for Criminology and Criminal Justice* (American Sociological Association Teaching Resources Center, 1984) and *Ideology and Controversy in the Classroom* (published as a special issue of the *Quarterly Journal of Ideology* and distributed as a teaching monograph by the American Sociological Association Teaching Resources Center, 1985).

JOSEPH J. WYDEVEN is an Associate Professor and Chair of the Department of English/Communication Arts at Bellevue College in Bellevue, Nebraska. He received his Ph.D. in American Studies and English from Purdue University in 1979. His publications include several essays on the photography and fiction of Wright Morris and on American Indian art. Professor Wydeven has been Chair of the Bellevue College Excellence in Teaching Committee since its inception in 1982.